WORDS OF WAID

INSPIRED BY THE CREATION ENERGY TEACHINGS
OF BILLY MEIER

Written By
Waid Sainvil

About The Author

My name is Waid Sainvil, and I was born and raised in Port-au-Prince, Haiti.

Coming from an Episcopalian family, attending church every Sunday was a regular part of my upbringing.

However, even from a young age, I found religion perplexing.

I couldn't grasp why a God, who supposedly created the universe effortlessly, would need money.

It deeply troubled me to see poor people sacrificing their meager earnings for the church while the pastor seemed to live a comfortable life, with his children receiving education abroad.

Meanwhile, I was always fascinated by the stars at night. I spent countless hours gazing at them from my rooftop. I used to play a game of guessing which one is home.

By the time I was 14, I had stopped attending my church and began exploring other religious denominations, hoping to find a more satisfying spiritual truth.

Over a period of 6 months, I attended Catholic, Jehovah's Witness, and Methodist services, as well as voodoo ceremonies, but they all seemed like intricate nonsense to me.

Still, I felt a persistent inner call urging me to seek the truth. As I grew older, my quest for spiritual fulfillment continued.

I explored Islam and Buddhism at different points in my life, yet neither provided the answers I sought.

I delved deeply into the New Age movement, reading countless books and following various gurus, but the search for truth remained unfulfilled.

It wasn't until I stumbled upon a YouTube video by Randolph featuring Billy Meier that I found something profoundly intriguing.

The compelling UFO photographs and contact reports by Meier captivated me, prompting an intense period of research and self-study.

Over the next two years, I immersed myself in daily reading and investigation, gradually realizing that Billy Meier's teachings resonated with the truth I had been seeking since childhood.

His scientific proofs and insights aligned with my quest, leading me to dedicate myself to his teachings.

Since then, I have learned a great deal, and I now consider these teachings to be the most significant aspect of life.

The journey to uncover this truth has been long and winding, but discovering Billy's work has brought immense clarity to those who found them.

It is my absolute hope that all my fellow Earth humans will also start benefiting from it.

Acknowledgments

I owe a tremendous debt of gratitude to Billy Meier for his guidance through these teachings.

His wisdom has been instrumental in my journey toward becoming a better human being.

Through his teachings, I have learned to cultivate inner peace and live in harmony with those around me.

For this, I am deeply thankful and forever indebted to his contributions to my personal growth.

In addition to Billy Meier, I must extend my heartfelt thanks

to Michael Voigtlaender. His encouragement was the spark that inspired me to write this book.

Without his support and understanding of the importance of sharing my experiences, this book might never have come to fruition.

His inspiration has been a crucial part of my journey, and I am immensely grateful for his influence.

My deepest appreciation also goes to my beautiful wife, Amber Dunlop, whose unwavering support has been a cornerstone throughout this process.

Her constant encouragement and trust in me have provided the strength and motivation needed to complete this book.

Amber's support has been invaluable, and I am profoundly thankful for her presence in my life.

I also want to acknowledge my three children, Audrey Simone, Kaz, and Jada, and express my dedication to creating a better world for them and for their future generations.

Next, I would like to express my gratitude to the FIGU community. Their love and brotherhood have been a source of comfort and inspiration. The sense of community and shared purpose I have found within FIGU is something I will cherish forever.

Last but not least, I would like to thank my wonderful next-door neighbor, Rodrigo Tintor, who worked tirelessly to help me put this book together in a PDF file in record time.

I am forever grateful for your help and support.

PREFACE

I am writing this book to share how the Creation Energy Teachings introduced by Billy Meier have profoundly transformed my life.

These teachings have freed me from the constant anxiety about the afterlife, allowing me to live genuinely and openly in every aspect of my existence.

By embracing these teachings, I have experienced a significant shift toward inner peace and reduced aggression.

They have provided me with clarity about the purpose of my life and the reason for my existence.

One of the most significant impacts of these teachings has been on my sense of purpose. I now have a clear understanding of why I am here and what I am meant to do.

This newfound clarity has been both liberating and empowering, enabling me to approach life with confidence and a deep sense of fulfillment.

The teachings have served as a guiding light, helping me navigate life's challenges with grace and resilience.

Although the words in this book are mine, they are deeply rooted in the Creation Energy Teachings brought to us by the Herald of the Universe, Billy Meier.

TABLE OF CONTENTS

Meeting Billy The First Time

When I mention meeting Billy, I'm often asked questions about our conversations and how accessible he is.

People are curious about what we discussed and whether it's easy to meet him.

Billy Meier is an exceptionally private individual who avoids the limelight and resists any form of idolization or fame.

Because of his preference for privacy, only a select few are aware of him at present. This deliberate seclusion adds to the mystique surrounding his persona.

Visiting the center in Switzerland where Billy resides offers occasional glimpses of him.

You might see him through a window or have a casual encounter in the kitchen, but such moments are always respectful and free from any starstruck behavior.

Everyone at the center maintains a level of decorum that aligns with Billy's desire for a low profile.

During my first encounter with Billy, he greeted me warmly despite his reserved nature.

Our conversation was straightforward, exchanging pleasantries about my background.

His humility and approachability were striking, as he maintained a gentle smile throughout.

WORDS OF WAID

Even when I sneezed due to allergies, his kindness and smile remained unwavering, making the interaction memorable and heartwarming.

For the rest of my stay that year, we developed a habit of waving at each other whenever our paths crossed, turning it into a friendly game.

These moments with Billy, even brief, left a profound impact on me, filling me with joy and a sense of equality.

In 2023, during another visit to the center, I saw him walking by, but we didn't get a chance to talk, likely due to COVID precautions.

Can hardly wait to see him again and to express my gratitude to him face-to-face: "Thank you! Thank you! And thank you!

HEALING A WOUND

To heal a wound effectively, it is essential to avoid touching it.

Constant interference with a healing wound can disrupt the natural healing process, potentially leading to complications.

Allowing the body to mend itself without interference is crucial for optimal recovery.

In the same way, emotional wounds also require a hands-off approach to allow for natural healing.

Humans often find a peculiar satisfaction in experiencing pain, using it as a means to indulge in self-pity.

This behavior, although seemingly comforting, can actually be quite detrimental.

By focusing on their suffering, individuals may seek validation or sympathy from others, but this only serves to reinforce their pain and hinder their recovery.

Pain deeply impacts both the psyche and the immune system.

When individuals dwell on their pain, it can lead to a cycle of negative thoughts and emotions, which in turn can weaken their overall health.

Chronic stress and emotional distress are known to have adverse effects on the body's ability to fight off illness and recover from injuries.

It is unwise to dwell in the past, as this only serves to remind us of what is gone and cannot be reclaimed.

WORDS OF WAID

Thoughts of lost loved ones, while natural, should not dominate one's mental landscape.

Constantly revisiting these memories only inflicts further pain upon oneself, preventing emotional healing.

Instead, focusing on the present and fostering new positive experiences can aid in moving forward and finding peace.

THE EAGLE

In the intricate landscape of US politics, one can see for themselves that both major parties represent different wings of the same Eagle.

Regardless of the party in power, the ultimate goal remains the same—to soar higher and higher.

However, this pursuit of power, influence and hegemony tendencies is not without its risks.

While Republicans and Democrats may espouse differing ideologies and policies, they are united in their quest for political supremacy.

This unity in ambition reflects the relentless nature of the Eagle's flight, driven by the desire to ascend to greater heights.

Yet, this singular focus on ascent can blind both parties to the potential consequences of their actions.

THE CONTACT REPORTS

The Contact Reports operate akin to a labyrinthine puzzle book, its enigmatic clues strewn across its pages awaiting discovery.

To embark on this journey, patience is a virtue, as each report demands thorough perusal, a minimum of three readings to unveil its hidden intricacies.

As you delve deeper into the text, connecting the scattered clues, the fog of ambiguity begins to lift, gradually unveiling a clearer, albeit fragmented, picture.

It is through this meticulous process of piecing together the puzzle that the overarching narrative emerges. Though initially obscured, clarity eventually dawns.

With each revelation, the disparate elements coalesce into a cohesive whole, transforming the once bewildering maze of information into a comprehensible tapestry of insight.

The journey is not without its surprises, as unexpected connections and revelations emerge from the depths of the text. Yet, as comprehension takes root, the once perplexing becomes lucid, guiding those with discerning eyes toward a deeper understanding of the intricate web of knowledge woven within the Contact Reports.

The quest to decipher these cryptic messages is a testament to the power of perseverance and the rewards it yields. Through diligent study and unwavering dedication, the pieces of the puzzle fall into place, revealing a panorama of wisdom and revelation.

Let those with the insight to perceive embark on this odyssey of discovery, for within the pages of the Contact Reports lies a treasure trove of enlightenment waiting to be unearthed.

KNOWLEDGE

To me, knowledge should be shared by all, motivating me to freely impart everything I've learned.

This principle stems from a fundamental desire not to hold knowledge as a means of elevation above others.

Rather, I see knowledge as a communal resource meant to enrich and empower all people equally.

In my worldview, the pursuit of knowledge isn't about personal gain or superiority but about collective growth and understanding.

By sharing what I know, I strive to contribute to a more equitable distribution of knowledge, ensuring that everyone has access to the insights and information that can enhance their lives and broaden their perspectives.

This ethos guides my interactions and collaborations, fostering an environment of openness and collaboration rather than competition or exclusivity.

I think that when knowledge is freely exchanged, barriers dissolve, and opportunities for learning and innovation flourish, benefitting society as a whole.

My commitment to sharing knowledge reflects a deep-seated understanding of the inherent worth and dignity of every individual.

By empowering others with the knowledge I possess, I hope to foster a world where everyone has the opportunity to thrive and contribute their unique talents and perspectives.

In the journey of life

In the journey of life, one essential truth stands unwavering: your resilience knows no bounds, not even in the face of mortality.

Encounters with death have been numerous, rendering enumeration futile.

Yet, the essence of this truth often eludes amidst the veils of religious doctrines designed to exert control through the fear of eternal consequences.

However, a solitary moment of introspection can unveil this verity, often obscured by the constructs of organized religion.

Tragically, for many, these dogmas serve as formidable mental barricades, obscuring the innate power within.

Let these words serve as an anthem of empowerment, urging you to navigate life's terrain with unwavering courage.

Within you lies an inexhaustible reservoir of strength, waiting to be unleashed upon the world.

Know that in every trial, every tribulation, you possess the fortitude to persevere.

My earnest encouragement stands behind you, a beacon of unwavering support, as you venture forth fearlessly into the unknown.

Cast aside the shackles of fear and doubt, for they are but illusions that veil the brilliance of your potential.

Embrace the freedom that comes with acknowledging your own resilience, transcending the limitations imposed by external influences.

In the absence of fear, you emerge as a force to be reckoned with, empowered to chart your own destiny amidst life's tumultuous currents.

May these words resonate within you as a reminder of your indomitable spirit, capable of weathering any storm that crosses your path.

Live boldly, for the universe awaits the unveiling of your boundless strength.

Remember, you are not alone in this journey—We stand beside you, a steadfast ally in your pursuit of a life lived without fear - Teamproud!

CREATION BEAUTY

The profound experience unveils the boundless beauty of Creation, surpassing all other forms of beauty.

It embodies limitless, profound happiness, an essence brimming with wisdom, knowledge, and truth.

This beauty is absolute, distinct, and eternal, resonating with intense vibrancy.

Its presence is not confined to external manifestations but resides within each human being as their Spirit-form or Creation Energy.

Within every human being, this essence of Creation dwells, pulsating with life and vitality.

It is the core of one's being, imbuing them with a sense of purpose and connection to the universe.

Regardless of external appearances or circumstances, every person carries within them this intrinsic beauty, reflecting the infinite magnificence of Creation itself.

Thus, the perception of beauty extends beyond mere physical attributes or surface-level qualities.

It encompasses the depth of one's spirit, the radiance of their inner essence.

In recognizing this universal truth, one comes to understand that every individual, in their unique expression of Creation Energy, is inherently beautiful.

Through this lens, beauty transcends the limitations of judgment or comparison, embracing the inherent worth and dignity of each person.

It is a celebration of the divine presence within every soul, a recognition of the interconnectedness and unity that binds all of humanity together in the tapestry of Creation's infinite splendor.

Bob Marley

The previously used formula for calculating the duration of time one's Creation Energy spends in the beyond before reincarnation was as follows: Age of death multiplied by

1.52 equals the time in the beyond.

However, due to overpopulation, Creation Energies are reincarnating sooner, rendering this formula obsolete.

Now, let's assess whether the Creation Energy of Bob Marley has reincarnated. Without considering overpopulation, the calculation would be 36 multiplied by 1.52, resulting in 55.

However, considering the years from 1981 to 2024, which totals 43, the difference is merely 12 years.

This suggests there may indeed be a child growing up in Miami, where he passed away, unaware of their connection to the legendary Bob Marley.

In the future, we will possess the capability to identify which Creation Energies are undergoing reincarnation.

Reincarnation stands as an undeniable truth.

SAME PLANET

We cohabit on the same planet, yet our struggle for harmonious living persists—a fundamental challenge.

Even within the construct of a single nation, we find ourselves fragmented by countless categories and subdivisions.

Surprisingly, divisions endure even within the supposedly strongest bonds of family ties.

Despite our perceived advancements, our mindset often mirrors that of ancient societies, fixated on the interests of smaller factions— the primitive mentality of small clans.

This behavior extends its reach into every facet of life, including the workplace, underscoring our lack of full awareness of this reality.

True peace can only emerge when we, as inhabitants of Earth, evolve sufficiently to recognize our collective identity and embrace our responsibility to care for one another, acknowledging that we are part of a unified human family, existing in a cohesive "We."

Thus lies the undeniable truth.

Logic

In a world dominated by beliefs, logic takes a back seat.

Beliefs are deeply ingrained convictions that people hold, often without evidence or rationality.

They shape how individuals perceive reality and make decisions, often overriding logical reasoning.

In such a world, emotions, traditions, and cultural norms often hold more sway than logical arguments.

This dynamic creates a challenging environment for those who rely on logic and reason to navigate through life.

In a world where beliefs reign supreme, logical arguments may fall on deaf ears or be dismissed outright.

People tend to interpret information in a way that confirms their existing beliefs rather than objectively evaluating evidence.

Despite the challenges, there are still opportunities to introduce logical thinking into a world dominated by beliefs.

By fostering critical thinking skills and encouraging open-mindedness, individuals can begin to question their own beliefs and those of others.

However, breaking through deeply entrenched beliefs requires patience, empathy, and a willingness to engage in meaningful dialogue.

Proving

Proving anything to a human being is akin to attempting to capture the wind in a net. Despite our best efforts, the essence of human free will remains unyielding. It's a fundamental aspect of our existence, imbuing each individual with the power to accept or reject any evidence presented to them.

No matter how compelling the argument or how robust the evidence is, the final judgment rests in the domain of human volition.

This inherent autonomy grants humans the ability to navigate through a sea of information, filtering, interpreting, and ultimately deciding what to accept as truth. In this process, evidence serves merely as a guidepost rather than a definitive determinant.

Each person constructs their own framework of belief, shaped not only by external evidence but also by internal biases, emotions, and experiences.

Attempts to persuade or convince others often encounter resistance, as the sovereignty of individual choice reigns supreme.Even the most incontrovertible evidence can be dismissed or rationalized away in the face of deeply held beliefs or preconceptions.

Thus, the notion of proving something to a human being becomes a complex interplay of logic, emotion, and perception.

In acknowledging the profound influence of free will, we embrace the inherent diversity of human thought and belief. Rather than seeking absolute certainty or universal agreement, we recognize the richness of human experience and the complexity of individual perspectives.

In this realization, we find humility and respect for the autonomy that defines us as human beings.

THE TRUTH

The truth is an unwavering force that cannot be suppressed indefinitely.

Despite attempts to conceal it, it inevitably rises to the surface, becoming unmistakable even to the most doubtful minds.

No amount of effort to obscure it can withstand the relentless persistence of truth.

Over time, the veil of deception is lifted, and the undeniable clarity of truth emerges. Its evidence becomes overwhelming, leaving no room for skepticism or disbelief.

Even the staunchest skeptics are compelled to recognize its existence in the face of overwhelming proof.

Letting truth guide our actions illuminates the path forward, serving as a beacon of clarity and righteousness.

Embracing truth leads to genuine peace, untainted by falsehoods or deceit. In its purity, truth offers a sanctuary where authentic peace and understanding can flourish.

Only by doing so can we begin to dismantle the structures of racism and move toward true equality and justice for all.

THE WHITE GOD

Imagine being told that God is black and that every other race on the planet accepts this belief without question.

As a black person, wouldn't you naturally feel a sense of superiority? This scenario mirrors the feelings of superiority some white people experience.

The roots of racism don't lie solely within individuals; rather, they stem from the beliefs ingrained in our society.

Racism is perpetuated through these deeply held beliefs.

By collectively accepting the image of a white god as the supreme being, we all play a part in sustaining systemic racism and white supremacy.

This acceptance reinforces a racial hierarchy, embedding the notion of white superiority into the fabric of our culture.

We all contribute to this system, often unconsciously, by not challenging these established norms.

The depiction of divinity as white isn't just a benign cultural choice. It's a powerful symbol that upholds racial biases and inequalities.

By not questioning this portrayal, we perpetuate a cycle of discrimination and prejudice.

In essence, the complicity in maintaining these beliefs makes us all guilty.

It's crucial to recognize and address these biases within ourselves and our society.

Wishing There Was a God

There are times when I find myself wishing for the existence of a god.

Imagine the freedom it would bring—I could engage in any criminal activity and simply ask for divine forgiveness afterward.

With a quick plea to a celestial father figure, all my transgressions would be wiped clean without the necessity of learning from my mistakes.

My sins would be absolved, and personal responsibility would become obsolete. How convenient would that be?

I especially yearn for a god when I'm facing unemployment and the daunting task of job hunting.

Instead of tirelessly searching for work, I could just remain at home, confident that a benevolent deity would provide for all my needs.

No effort is required on my part—a divine safety net ensuring my well-being. That sounds like an incredible arrangement.

During tornado season, the desire for a god grows even stronger.

Residing in a tornado alley, I could simply beseech the Lord to spare my home from the ravages of nature.

The assurance of divine intervention would bring immense peace of mind. Like many others, I find myself wishing for the comfort and security that belief in a god might bring.

However, the stark reality is that no such deity exists. We are solely responsible for our lives, our actions, and the consequences that follow.

LIFE IS ETERNAL

Life is an eternal continuum, encompassing the essence of existence in all forms. The creation energy that resides within human beings, animals, and plants is the very essence of life itself.

This energy is what animates and sustains all living things, connecting every part of the natural world in a shared experience of existence.

Death should be understood not as an end but as a natural counterpart to birth, the two sides of the same coin that we call life.

Just as birth marks the beginning of our journey, death represents a transition, a return to the cycle that perpetuates life. This cyclical nature underscores the continuity of life rather than its cessation.

Reincarnation is a fundamental aspect of this eternal cycle, a process by which life renews itself. The concept of reincarnation offers a perspective that life does not simply end with death but transforms and continues in different forms.

This understanding can profoundly affect how we perceive our existence, alleviating the fear of death and allowing us to embrace life more fully.

By recognizing that we have lived and died countless times, we can free ourselves from the existential anxieties that often stem from fear of the unknown. This awareness helps us to live more freely, unburdened by the dread of what lies beyond death.

In acknowledging our place in the continuous flow of life, we come to see ourselves as part of a larger, enduring lineage, carrying forward the legacy of our ancestors.

RELEARN

Earth humans must come to a profound realization. We need to re-evaluate and let go of everything we have always believed to be true.

Our current knowledge and understanding are built on a foundation of beliefs, many of which are fundamentally flawed or untrue.

This recognition is crucial because these beliefs are often based on limited perceptions, cultural biases, and misinformation.

To truly advance and grow, humans must engage in a rigorous process of unlearning.

This means critically examining and dismantling the assumptions and misconceptions that have shaped our worldview. It requires a willingness to question long-held notions and to recognize the limitations of our current understanding.

Once humans have cleared away the old, outdated beliefs, we can embark on the path of learning anew.

This new learning involves seeking knowledge with an open mind, embracing uncertainty, and valuing evidence and reason over preconceived ideas.

It is a continuous process of growth and adaptation, where every new piece of information is weighed and considered in the light of a broader, more nuanced perspective.

The journey ahead for Earth humans is one of profound transformation. We must unlearn what we think we know and be open to learning from a place of genuine curiosity and humility.

This shift in perspective is essential for uncovering deeper truths and achieving a more enlightened state of understanding.

Only by letting go of our outdated beliefs and embracing a more open, inquisitive approach can we hope to navigate the complexities of the world and our place within it.

This transformation requires courage and dedication, but it is the path to a more profound and authentic comprehension of ourselves and the universe.

Through this journey of unlearning and relearning, we can aspire to create a more informed, compassionate, and enlightened society.

KNOW THYSELF

Contrary to what you've been told, never simply believe in yourself. Blind belief can lead you astray, creating a false sense of confidence that may not be grounded in reality.

Instead of relying on unexamined faith in your abilities, focus on a deeper understanding of who you are.

You need to know yourself. Self-awareness is the foundation of genuine growth and success.

It involves an honest assessment of your strengths and weaknesses, aspirations and fears.

By truly knowing yourself, you can make more informed decisions that align with your values and goals.

When you understand yourself, you can navigate life's challenges with greater clarity and purpose.

Knowing your limits and recognizing areas for improvement allows you to seek out the necessary resources and support.

This self-knowledge helps you set realistic goals and create effective strategies to achieve them, avoiding the pitfalls of overconfidence or self-deception.

Knowing yourself is more empowering than merely believing in yourself. It grounds your confidence in reality and equips you with the insight needed to grow and adapt.

This deeper understanding fosters resilience and authenticity, enabling you to pursue your true potential with a clear and focused mind.

FEAR OF GOD

I do not fear any man, nor do I fear any god. This statement reflects a profound understanding of where true power and influence lie—not in external entities or forces but within ourselves.

When we relinquish the fear of the external, we can focus on the internal struggles that truly shape our lives.

It is essential for us to understand that our greatest adversary lies within ourselves. This internal adversary is often far more challenging to confront than any external opponent.

It is composed of the fears, doubts, and negative self-beliefs that reside in our minds and hearts.

These internal struggles can be insidious, quietly undermining our confidence and sense of self-worth.

The obstacles and challenges we face are often self-imposed, stemming from our own doubts, insecurities, and inner conflicts.

These self-imposed barriers can manifest in various ways, such as procrastination, self-sabotage, and the reluctance to take risks. They are born from past experiences, societal pressures, and our internal dialogue.

Understanding this allows us to see that the power to change our circumstances lies within our own grasp.Recognizing this truth is the first step toward overcoming the internal barriers that hold us back.

By identifying and acknowledging these internal obstacles, we begin the journey toward self-mastery.

This process involves introspection, self-compassion, and the willingness to face our deepest fears. It is through this inner work that we can dismantle the barriers that prevent us from reaching our full potential.

Achieving true self-mastery over our own lives is a profound and empowering experience.

It means taking full responsibility for our actions, decisions, and emotions. It involves cultivating a mindset of growth and resilience, where challenges are seen as opportunities for learning and development.

When we master our inner world, we unlock the ability to create a fulfilling and purposeful life free from the constraints of fear and self-doubt.

HEARTBREAK

Embrace the possibility of heartbreak, as these experiences often impart the most profound lessons. While the pain of a broken heart can be intense, it also serves as a catalyst for growth and self-discovery.

Through heartbreak, we learn more about our resilience, capacity for love, and the depth of our emotional strength. Heartbreaks challenge us to reflect on our relationships and ourselves, offering invaluable insights that can shape our future interactions.

These painful moments encourage us to examine our desires, boundaries, and what we truly need from our connections with others.

This self-awareness paves the way for healthier and more fulfilling relationships in the future.

Moreover, experiencing heartbreak fosters empathy and understanding. As we navigate our own emotional turmoil, we become more attuned to the struggles and vulnerabilities of others.

This heightened sensitivity can deepen our compassion, making us more supportive and considerate partners, friends, and family members. The lessons learned from heartbreak contribute to our personal evolution.

Each experience, no matter how painful, adds to our emotional resilience and wisdom.

By facing heartbreak head-on and embracing the growth it offers, we emerge stronger, more self-aware, and better equipped to build meaningful and lasting relationships in the future.

EQUAL VALUE II

It's essential to let go of any sense of self-importance, recognizing that all humans possess equal value. Elevating oneself above others fosters division and hinders genuine connection.

Embracing humility and equality allows us to appreciate the inherent worth of every individual, fostering mutual respect and understanding.

When we acknowledge the equal value of all people, we create an environment that promotes inclusivity and empathy.

Each person brings unique experiences and perspectives that contribute to the rich tapestry of our shared human experience.

By valuing others as equals, we open ourselves to learning and growing from the diverse insights and talents that everyone has to offer.

Moreover, refraining from self-importance helps us build stronger, more authentic relationships. When we approach others with humility and respect, we break down barriers and cultivate trust.

This foundation of mutual respect enables more meaningful and constructive interactions, enhancing our ability to collaborate and support one another in meaningful ways.

Embracing the principle of equal value among all humans enriches our lives and strengthens our communities.

By recognizing that no one is inherently superior or inferior, we pave the way for a more compassionate and just society.

This mindset encourages us to treat others with kindness and fairness, fostering a world where everyone has the opportunity to thrive and contribute to the greater good.

Meeting Billy the 2nd time

During my last visit to the center, I learned a very valuable lesson. We are all equal in value.

While having a small talk with Billy, I was just about to express how happy I was.

Before I could start, he quickly shushed me and proceeded to tell us what needed to be done in the garden.

He dislikes receiving praise.

Reflecting on it, I now understand his perspective. We're all equal.

He doesn't want to be placed on a pedestal like the gurus and the men of god.

That's why only a few know about him and share his teachings here on Facebook and other media platforms.

In that visit, I learned more than I ever could from reading his books. Because he, himself, is the Goblet of the Truth.

THE JOY OF BEING WRONG

Embracing the realization of being wrong is a catalyst for personal growth and evolution. Unlike the static certainty of being right, acknowledging one's mistakes opens the door to learning and development.

Every instance of being wrong serves as an opportunity to expand our understanding, refine our perspectives, and ultimately evolve as individuals.

The humility that comes with admitting one's fallibility fosters a mindset of continuous improvement. Rather than clinging to rigid beliefs or defending our ego, embracing our errors allows us to adopt a more fluid and adaptable approach to life.

Through the process of acknowledging and learning from our mistakes, we gain invaluable insights that propel us forward on our journey of self-discovery and growth.

Moreover, the willingness to accept being wrong cultivates resilience and resilience in the face of adversity. Instead of viewing mistakes as failures, we see them as stepping stones towards greater insight and understanding.

This shift in perspective empowers us to confront challenges with courage and determination, knowing that every setback is an opportunity for growth and transformation.

Undoubtedly, the love for being wrong stems from a deep appreciation for the beauty of the human experience. It is through our fallibility that we discover our capacity for growth, empathy, and resilience.

WORDS OF WAID

By embracing the lessons inherent in our mistakes, we unlock the door to endless possibilities and embark on a journey of self-discovery and evolution.

COMMUNICATION AND UNDERSTANDING

Communication serves as the bedrock upon which strong relationships are built, and harmonious communities thrive.

However, despite its paramount importance, various obstacles often impede our ability to truly connect with one another.

Miscommunication, misunderstandings, assumptions, and premature conclusions frequently derail meaningful interactions, hindering the establishment of genuine connections.

Ironically, individuals who share common values and ideals can find themselves at odds due to a lack of understanding and empathy.

This underscores the critical need for active listening, open-mindedness, and a genuine willingness to engage in constructive dialogue.

Only through empathetic listening can we truly comprehend the perspectives and experiences of others, fostering mutual understanding and empathy.

It is imperative that individuals cultivate a habit of listening intently to their fellow human beings.

By actively listening, we create an environment where voices are heard and genuine understanding can flourish.

This approach enables us to dismantle barriers, resolve conflicts, and collaborate toward the realization of a more compassionate and inclusive society.

While life itself may not be inherently complicated, our differences and misunderstandings often obscure its simplicity.

WORDS OF WAID

By placing empathy, understanding, and effective communication at the forefront of our interactions, we can navigate complexities with greater ease.

Through prioritizing these principles, we pave the way for simpler, more harmonious interactions, thereby contributing to the creation of a more cohesive and compassionate world, one conversation at a time.

The More One Understands

As your understanding deepens, a profound cycle of comprehension unfolds, leading to further enlightenment.

With each layer of understanding that is peeled back, new insights emerge, fueling a continuous process of comprehension.

This iterative journey of understanding leads to a heightened awareness and clarity of thought, allowing you to grasp complex concepts with greater ease and depth.

As you delve deeper into the realms of knowledge and insight, the interconnectedness of ideas becomes increasingly apparent.

Each nugget of understanding serves as a building block, laying the foundation for the acquisition of further knowledge.

Through this interconnected web of comprehension, disparate pieces of information coalesce into a cohesive tapestry of understanding, illuminating the intricate workings of the world around us.

Moreover, as your understanding expands, so too does your capacity for critical thinking and analysis.

Armed with a broader perspective and a deeper understanding of underlying principles, you are better equipped to navigate the complexities of life and make informed decisions.

This heightened level of comprehension empowers you to approach challenges with confidence and resourcefulness, drawing upon a wealth of knowledge and insight to overcome obstacles.

The pursuit of understanding is a lifelong journey characterized by continuous growth and discovery.

WORDS OF WAID

With each step forward, you inch closer to the pinnacle of comprehension, gaining new perspectives and insights along the way.

By embracing this journey with humility and curiosity, you open yourself up to a world of possibilities where the pursuit of knowledge is both a noble endeavor and a rewarding pursuit.

Interaction and Lesson

Within every interaction lies a valuable lesson waiting to be uncovered.

It is incumbent upon us to discern the significance of these lessons and glean wisdom from our experiences.

Each encounter, whether positive or negative, offers an opportunity for growth and self-reflection.

By approaching interactions with an open mind and a willingness to learn, we can extract valuable insights that contribute to our personal development and understanding of the world around us.

The ability to recognize the lessons inherent in our interactions empowers us to derive meaning from even the most mundane encounters.

Every conversation, encounter, or exchange of ideas has the potential to broaden our perspective and deepen our understanding of ourselves and others.

By paying attention to the subtleties of human interaction and reflecting on our experiences, we can uncover profound truths about life, relationships, and the human condition.

Moreover, embracing the notion that every interaction carries a lesson fosters a mindset of curiosity and inquiry.

Instead of merely reacting to our experiences, we can approach them with a sense of curiosity and openness, eager to uncover the deeper meaning beneath the surface.

WORDS OF WAID

This mindset encourages us to engage with the world around us more consciously, seeking out opportunities for growth and learning in every interaction we have.

The practice of recognizing and learning from the lessons inherent in our interactions enriches our lives and enhances our understanding of ourselves and the world.

By embracing the wisdom that emerges from our experiences, we can navigate life's challenges with greater resilience and insight, continually evolving and growing as individuals.

THE HERALD

The Herald, a figure veiled in mystery and transcendence, wielded his bow with an ethereal grace, drawing it back with unwavering purpose.

His arrows, not forged of steel, but rather composed of profound truths and wisdom, were released into the world with unparalleled precision.

They soared through the realm of ignorance, piercing the veil of falsehoods that clouded the minds of humanity.

Though his physical presence remained hidden from mortal eyes, the impact of his words reverberated through hearts and souls, leaving an indelible mark on the collective consciousness.

The Herald's essence, elusive and enigmatic, remained forever intertwined with the fabric of truth, forever guiding and enlightening, even in his unseen form.

I Don't Pray

I abstain from prayer because I possess a clear understanding of my desires and aspirations.

Rather than seeking guidance or assistance through prayer, I choose to rely on my own introspection and determination to pursue what I want in life.

This self-assurance allows me to navigate my journey with confidence and clarity, trusting in my own abilities and decisions to manifest my goals and aspirations.

SINGLE LIFE

Societal norms and traditional expectations often dictate that individuals should pursue romantic relationships regardless of their personal desires or inclinations.

This pressure can lead many people to enter into relationships that may not align with their authentic selves simply to conform to societal standards.

Consequently, individuals may find themselves in partnerships that feel forced or unnatural.

On the other hand, those who consciously choose to embrace a single life may face scrutiny and judgment from others who subscribe to conventional beliefs about relationships.

Even those who confidently opt for singledom may experience moments of doubt or insecurity when confronted with external opinions and expectations.

The pervasive influence of societal norms can cast doubt on the validity of their choice, leading them to question their own happiness and fulfillment.

It is crucial to recognize that every individual possesses the inherent right to shape their own life according to their own values and preferences.

Choosing to remain single and finding contentment in one's own company is a legitimate and empowering decision that should be respected and celebrated.

Whether one embraces singlehood, partnership, or any other lifestyle, the key is authenticity and alignment with one's true self.

WORDS OF WAID

Single life offers its own unique beauty and opportunities for growth, just as coupled life does.

Each individual has the autonomy to define their own path and find fulfillment on their own terms.

Society's expectations should not dictate the validity or worthiness of someone's life choices.

Instead, true empowerment comes from embracing one's authentic self and living in alignment with one's own truth, regardless of societal pressures or judgments.

LIFE IS ETERNAL

Life transcends the boundaries of time and space, existing in a perpetual cycle of creation and transformation.

Within every living being, from humans to animals and plants, pulses the essence of life itself – a vibrant energy that sustains existence and propels evolution forward.

Birth and death are merely two facets of the same eternal continuum, each marking a transition in the journey of life.

In this cosmic dance of existence, reincarnation emerges as a fundamental truth.

The soul traverses the realms of existence, experiencing myriad lifetimes in an endless quest for growth and enlightenment.

Reincarnation offers solace and understanding, freeing individuals from the shackles of fear and uncertainty surrounding death.

It affirms that the essence of life endures beyond physical form, perpetuating the cycle of existence across time and space.

Embracing the reality of reincarnation liberates the human spirit from existential angst and dogmatic beliefs about the afterlife.

It invites individuals to live authentically and fearlessly, unencumbered by the specter of death.

Recognizing the interconnectedness of all beings across the vast expanse of time, individuals find solace in the knowledge that they are part of an eternal continuum – a tapestry of existence woven by countless lifetimes.

WORDS OF WAID

In this grand tapestry of life, every individual is but a thread woven into the fabric of existence by the collective experiences of past lives.

We are the culmination of our ancestors' hopes, dreams, and struggles, carrying their legacy forward into the ever-unfolding present.

Acknowledging our interconnectedness with the past, present, and future, we embrace the eternal nature of life and find meaning in our existence as we continue the timeless journey of evolution and growth.

Holding Doors

When you hold the door open for someone, their reaction should not be your primary concern.

It's important to remember that you cannot control how another person chooses to respond.

People have varied ways of expressing gratitude, or they might not express it at all, and that's perfectly fine.

The most crucial aspect to focus on is your own behavior. Your actions are a reflection of your values and character.

By choosing to be considerate, you are embodying the qualities you find important. This act of kindness is a testament to the type of person you aspire to be.

Whether the other person acknowledges your gesture or not does not diminish the value of your kindness. The true worth lies in the fact that you acted with integrity and thoughtfulness.

Your decision to be kind is significant in itself, regardless of external validation.

Moreover, such actions set a positive example for others. When people observe considerate behavior, they are more likely to act similarly.

By consistently being a positive example, you contribute to a more thoughtful and respectful community.

43

BEING TRUE TO ONESELF

The ultimate freedom lies in embracing one's true self and shedding the masks society often imposes. Authenticity allows individuals to express their genuine thoughts, feelings, and beliefs without fear of judgment or rejection.

By embracing authenticity, individuals liberate themselves from the constraints of societal expectations and cultivate a deeper sense of self-awareness and fulfillment.

However, when individuals hide behind masks and facades, they hinder genuine connections with others. Authentic relationships thrive on mutual understanding and acceptance, which can only occur when individuals reveal their true selves.

When people conceal their authentic identities, they rob themselves and others of the opportunity to truly know and connect with one another on a meaningful level.

Moreover, the lack of authenticity in interactions breeds disharmony and discontentment. When individuals present themselves inauthentically, they contribute to a culture of superficiality and distrust.

Genuine relationships require honesty and vulnerability, and without them, relationships become shallow and fragmented, leading to feelings of isolation and disconnection.

Embracing authenticity fosters harmony and peace within oneself and in relationships with others.

By embracing who we truly are, we create space for genuine connections and foster a sense of belonging and acceptance.

When individuals are free to be themselves without fear of judgment or rejection, they can cultivate deep, meaningful connections built on trust, understanding, and mutual respect.

Speaking Truth

The ultimate freedom lies in embracing one's true self and shedding the masks society often imposes.

Authenticity allows individuals to express their genuine thoughts, feelings, and beliefs without fear of judgment or rejection.

By embracing authenticity, individuals liberate themselves from the constraints of societal expectations and cultivate a deeper sense of self-awareness and fulfillment.

However, when individuals hide behind masks and facades, they hinder genuine connections with others.

Authentic relationships thrive on mutual understanding and acceptance, which can only occur when individuals reveal their true selves.

When people conceal their authentic identities, they rob themselves and others of the opportunity to truly know and connect with one another on a meaningful level.

Moreover, the lack of authenticity in interactions breeds disharmony and discontentment. When individuals present themselves inauthentically, they contribute to a culture of superficiality and distrust.

Genuine relationships require honesty and vulnerability, and without them, relationships become shallow and fragmented, leading to feelings of isolation and disconnection.

Embracing authenticity fosters harmony and peace within oneself and in relationships with others.

By embracing who we truly are, we create space for genuine connections and foster a sense of belonging and acceptance.

When individuals are free to be themselves without fear of judgment or rejection, they can cultivate deep, meaningful connections built on trust, understanding, and mutual respect.

Living Though Your Children

Living vicariously through your children is unfair to both you and them, fostering disharmony and unrest in the relationship dynamic.

When parents project their own unfulfilled aspirations onto their children, it places undue pressure on the young ones and can lead to feelings of inadequacy or resentment.

Children deserve the freedom to explore their own interests and passions without feeling burdened by their parents' expectations or unmet dreams.

When parents overly impose their desires onto their children, it stifles their individuality and inhibits their ability to develop a sense of self.

Furthermore, this dynamic can strain the parent-child relationship, as the child may feel misunderstood or controlled, while the parent may become frustrated if their expectations are not met.

It's essential for parents to nurture their children's autonomy and support them in pursuing their own paths rather than attempting to shape them into a reflection of themselves.

Fostering a relationship built on mutual respect, understanding, and encouragement allows both parent and child to thrive independently, fostering a sense of harmony and peace within the family unit.

Start The Day

Start your day by embracing positive thoughts and extending heartfelt good mornings to those around you.

Make a conscious effort to cultivate an environment infused with love and kindness.

Doing so not only nurtures the well-being of others but also reflects the love and compassion you harbor within yourself.

Keep in mind that the emotions you outwardly express are a reflection of your inner state. If anger is a frequent visitor in your interactions, it likely indicates a deeper reservoir of anger within you.

Redirect your focus towards fostering love and positivity. Not only will this improve your emotional well-being, but it will also contribute to creating a more harmonious atmosphere for everyone you encounter.

IMMORTALITY

Understanding human immortality has the potential to dismantle feelings of jealousy, envy, and greed, as individuals would recognize that this current life is not their final chapter.

Realizing that achievements and success in one lifetime benefit the collective existence of all beings could fundamentally shift perspectives and modes of thinking.

Truth, when embraced, has the power to profoundly reshape perceptions and ideologies, paving the way for the long-awaited peace on Earth.

The sooner humanity embraces this truth, the sooner peace will manifest.

THE TRUTH

The truth, donning its shoes, strides forward relentlessly, unstoppable and poised to sweep aside anything in its path.

Love And Time

Love transcending time is deeply profound and has been revered in myriad forms throughout human history, dating back to antiquity.

It speaks to the enduring nature of love and the profound connections that persist beyond the constraints of time.

Often described as "love at first sight," it embodies the belief in connections between individuals that surpass the boundaries of a single lifetime.

At its core, love in its purest form defies the limitations imposed by temporal constraints. Love, at first sight represents a profound and immediate recognition of a Creation Energy connection that predates the current lifetime.

It signifies a profound intertwining of destinies, where two souls recognize each other across the vast expanse of time.

Embracing the truth that our connections with others extend beyond the present moment can foster a deeper appreciation for the relationships we cultivate.

This awareness of the enduring nature of love may inspire a sense of responsibility and commitment to nurturing meaningful connections.

Moreover, acknowledging the timeless essence of love can encourage a broader, more compassionate view of humanity. Recognizing that the bonds we form with others are rooted in a timeless, interconnected tapestry can foster empathy and understanding.

It serves as a reminder that, despite the apparent differences that may divide us, there is a common thread of love that unites all of humanity.

Once again, we are truly interconnected as one.

CHRISTIANS AND MUSLIMS

To the esteemed members of the Christian and Muslim faiths,

I wish to convey a profound understanding regarding the Herald of this Universe, known as Henock/Nokodemion.

It's imperative to grasp that reincarnation does not entail the return of the same human form or personality.

Such a notion is fundamentally impossible.

While we respect your anticipation of their return, it's crucial to discern that expecting their reappearance in the likeness of past prophets like Jmmanuel (Jesus Christ) and Mohammed is misguided.

Rather, we bring to your attention that both emanate from the same Creation Energy and have reincarnated since February 3rd, 1937, under the name Billy, heralding the return of the Messenger.

It's evident that we are all united in our pursuit and allegiance to the same Messiah.

The distinction lies in the methodology: while you adhere to ancient scriptures that may have been tampered with due to the Herald's avoidance of written teachings during times of widespread illiteracy, I have recognized and embraced his current reincarnation and authentic teachings in this lifetime.

This recognition is an accomplishment I cherish deeply, as it necessitates extensive effort, inquiry, and introspection.

Nevertheless, our mission remains unchanged throughout the ages, and the teachings persist as timeless truths.

THE FINAL WAR

Presently, two dominant religious figures persist on Earth: the white God, represented by Jesus, and the Arab God, embodied by Mohammed.

This dichotomy fuels perpetual conflict in the Middle East, where these deities are believed to engage in a final battle.

It's worth noting that Nokodemion, reincarnated as Mohammed, aimed to counterbalance Christianity's global influence, foreseeing its dominance.

Mohammed successfully fulfills this mission, and now, as Billy, Nokodemion endeavors to eradicate both gods from humanity's collective consciousness, a task he is believed to accomplish.

Even within the realm of the white God, internal conflict brews, mirroring past events among the Plejaren beings who once inhabited Earth.

Two opposing forces, represented by China and Russia, are predicted to unite to curb the hegemonic tendencies of the USA, analogous to the unity between Ptaah and Salam, who exiled Arussem, driven by ambitions of power.

This collaboration is anticipated to bring about peace and the dissolution of the concept of God from the human mind.

To me, the parallels between Earth's unfolding events and those of the Plejaren civilization are unmistakable.

However, it's essential to clarify that these interpretations are only my personal views.

BELIEF IN GOD

Belief in God stems from doubt, prompting prayers born out of uncertainty. In such moments, one hopes to be heard by a higher power.

However, if certainty in God's existence is unwavering, the impulse to pray diminishes, as faith assures that needs are understood and provided for.

One alternative is to substitute the notion of God with an acknowledgment of inner strength and Creation Energy within oneself.

By recognizing oneself as a guiding force and one's own deity, belief shifts inward.

Once this truth is embraced, the need for belief fades, replaced by an eternal quest for knowledge and understanding.

STARS

Sometimes, what shines brightest is devoid of life. Consider the stars in the sky.

The stronger the desire to outshine others, the deeper the connection to materialism, which can cloud one's perception of their true essence as a Creation energy—a minuscule yet integral part of the Universal consciousness.

The ultimate purpose of this essence is to evolve through the acquisition of wisdom and knowledge.

Don't allow the allure of shiny objects to distract you from the genuine illumination of life.

Skepticism

The skeptics, we deeply value skepticism as a healthy and rational approach to understanding the world.

We respect and acknowledge your skepticism towards the Billy Meier case, as many of us within the community have also grappled with doubt.

However, skepticism shouldn't be a roadblock; instead, it should serve as a catalyst for further investigation.

Those who remain skeptical of Billy Meier often either lack the inclination to delve deeper or have already formed a fixed opinion, resulting in a repeated dismissal of the subject.

It's important to recognize that not everyone is immediately open to accepting new ideas, and that's perfectly acceptable.

On a personal level, I have chosen not to engage in arguments with skeptics anymore as I have progressed beyond that stage.

However, your opinions are still valued and welcomed, albeit with an understanding of our perspective.

It's crucial to note that none of us were pressured to "believe" in Billy Meier; rather, we each arrived at our own conclusions through extensive exploration.

For me, this journey entailed two years of daily reading, participation in Q&A forums, watching videos, and studying various materials.

So when we express that our minds cannot be changed, we genuinely mean it, having invested significant time and effort in forming our understanding.

ORGASM

Orgasm serves as a profound reminder of our connection to the origins of Creation.

To comprehend the state beyond, imagine the intensity of your most euphoric orgasm multiplied by a trillion. Therefore, there is no need to be afraid of death.

THE WORLD OF SPORTS

In the world of sports, the notion of a team goes beyond its physical players, existing instead in the collective imagination of its supporters.

This abstract concept embodies the loyalty, passion, and camaraderie that fans invest in their chosen team, regardless of individual player characteristics or identities.

It represents a shared spirit and ethos that unites people under a common banner.

Within this framework, a paradox emerges: individuals holding racist beliefs may still fervently support a team predominantly comprised of players from a race they discriminate against.

This apparent contradiction stems from fans separating the team entity from its individual members.

To them, the team symbolizes shared values, aspirations, and the pursuit of excellence, transcending the racial makeup of its players.

When fans watch their team in action, they don't see just a group of individuals but a cohesive unit united by a common purpose.

The players' diverse backgrounds, experiences, and identities are overshadowed by the collective identity of the team, forged through dedication, hard work, and mutual respect.

This unity demonstrates humanity's remarkable ability to overcome differences and unite as one, even amidst external challenges and prejudices.

Achieving such unity and love in sports gives hope for a future where similar harmony can prevail in society, leading to a world where humanity moves forward together as a unified force.

INFIDELITY

The phenomenon of infidelity among men often stems not from a lack of love or a desire to terminate a relationship but rather from the inherent aspect of polygamy encoded within their DNA.

This inclination towards multiple partners can be observed in various species in nature, such as the lion, which maintains a pride consisting of multiple lionesses.

Despite the presence of such thoughts, fidelity entails the conscious choice to refrain from acting upon these impulses—a testament to an individual's ability to exercise self- control and uphold the commitments of their relationship.

Acknowledging and accepting the natural inclination towards polygamy could potentially mitigate various societal issues, including high divorce rates, instances of domestic violence, emotional abuse, and even homicide rates.

Embracing polygamous relationships as a societal norm could lead to greater marital stability and harmony in the long run.

However, it is crucial to recognize that not everyone is predisposed to this lifestyle, and individuals retain the freedom to choose their own paths and relationship dynamics.

Just as individuals may be born into bodies that do not align with their gender identity due to their DNA makeup, the inclination towards infidelity among men is also attributed to biological factors.

Moreover, with reincarnation, individuals experience life in various genders across different lifetimes, emphasizing the fluidity and complexity of human experiences.

WORDS OF WAID

In essence, what is deemed acceptable or natural for one gender in a lifetime is also extended to the other one in the next lifetime, fostering a more equitable and inclusive understanding of human behavior and relationships.

Believers

Believers often attribute all events, whether fortunate or tragic, to the benevolence of a divine entity, absolving themselves of personal accountability.

They recount tales of divine intervention following miraculous escapes from perilous situations, extolling the greatness and mercy of their chosen deity.

However, this singular focus on divine providence overlooks the suffering and loss experienced by those who were not as fortunate, exposing a narrow-minded perspective that prioritizes individual salvation over collective empathy and human solidarity.

Such a mindset, rooted in religious dogma, undermines the fundamental essence of humanity and erodes our capacity for genuine connection and compassion.

While some may categorize me as religious, I refrain from identifying as such, as I only follow the Teachings of the Herald Billy, centered around the concept of Creation Energy.

Through embracing these teachings, I have transcended the confines of individual identity, recognizing myself as inseparable from the collective human experience.

In adopting this holistic perspective, I acknowledge the interconnectedness of all beings, viewing humanity not as a collection of separate entities but as a unified whole—a "We- form" in which each individual's joys and sorrows resonate with the collective consciousness.

WORDS OF WAID

Within this interconnected framework, the pain and suffering of one individual reverberate throughout the collective consciousness of humanity, eliciting a shared sense of empathy and compassion.

By embracing our interconnectedness and acknowledging the inherent worth and dignity of every individual, we cultivate a deeper sense of empathy and solidarity, fostering a more compassionate and inclusive society.

ELECTED OFFICIALS

The selection of individuals for positions of power within a society offers a profound reflection of its collective values, beliefs, and priorities.

Through the democratic process of elections or other forms of governance, society entrusts certain individuals with the responsibility of leadership, expecting them to embody and uphold the ideals that resonate with the broader populace.

The individuals elected into power often emerge from within the societal fabric, rising to prominence through various channels such as political parties, grassroots movements, or community activism.

As such, they are intimately acquainted with the hopes, fears, and aspirations of their constituents, making them a mirror of the society they represent.

Moreover, the policies and decisions enacted by those in power invariably shape the trajectory of the society as a whole, leaving an indelible imprint on its social, economic, and political landscape.

In this sense, the actions and behaviors of elected officials not only reflect the values of the society but also influence its future direction and development.

The relationship between those in power and the society they govern is symbiotic in nature, characterized by a constant exchange of influence and accountability.

As stewards of the public trust, elected officials bear the weighty responsibility of safeguarding the welfare and interests of the society they serve while simultaneously being held to account by the very individuals who bestowed upon them the mantle of leadership.

I am My Own God

Allow me to elucidate my perspective on identifying myself as my own god. To the uninitiated, this assertion may evoke notions of possessing supernatural abilities, such as moving mountains or foreseeing future events.

However, such interpretations miss the mark.

When I assert that I am my own god, it signifies my recognition of sole responsibility for my life's trajectory.

Every outcome, whether favorable or unfavorable, stems directly from the decisions I make. I am beholden to no external force, offering neither thanks nor blame but to myself.

This realization fosters a profound sense of agency and empowerment, enabling me to navigate life fearlessly, unshackled by apprehension or doubt.

Furthermore, I understand that the world I leave behind is the same world I shall inherit upon reincarnation.

Living a life devoid of beliefs, grounded solely in reality, does not preclude the possibility of extraordinary feats.

While I may not presently possess abilities akin to moving mountains or predicting lottery numbers, I acknowledge the potential for such feats within the realm of logical possibility.

At this stage of my consciousness, however, I am not equipped with such capabilities.

Creation operates according to logic—a principle that underscores the evolutionary journey of human consciousness.

As we evolve, our capacity for consciousness expands, akin to upgrading the software of a computer system.

The inability of most Earth humans to recall past lives stems from the limitations of their current consciousness level.

Our comprehension is confined by the bounds of our consciousness, necessitating multiple reincarnations to attain higher levels of understanding.

Exceptional individuals like Billy, whose consciousness surpasses conventional bounds, possess the rare ability to recall past lives.

His unparalleled Creation Energy, spanning 9.6 billion years, distinguishes him as the Herald—an embodiment of the highest consciousness within the human form.

In essence, while I acknowledge myself as my own god, I recognize that above me stands only Creation—the Universal Consciousness.

I am but a conduit through which its power flows, utilizing the highest level of consciousness available to me in this lifetime.

LIKE A COMPUTER

In the realm of computer systems, we encounter a fundamental dichotomy: Hardware and Software. Hardware encompasses the tangible, visible components of the system— the monitor, CPU, keyboard, and mouse—while Software comprises a set of instructions that enable the hardware to execute specific tasks with precision and efficiency.

Similarly, life serves as a classroom for Creation itself, a vast canvas upon which the process of evolution unfolds.

Through the medium of humanoid forms such as ourselves, Creation seeks to transcend and elevate its own existence, echoing the timeless principle of "As above, so below." We are but nascent creators at the early stages of our journey towards unlocking the boundless potential within.

Just as the inner workings of a system reflect its external manifestations, so too does the process of creation manifest both within and without.

To those endowed with the requisite software—the capacity for understanding and insight—these parallels become apparent.

They perceive the interconnectedness of all existence and recognize the profound significance of their role in the cosmic drama of evolution.

YOU'RE NOT THE BODY

You exist beyond the confines of your physical body. As you embark on the transition to the realm beyond, your mortal shell remains behind, destined to return to the elements from which it came.

Meanwhile, your essence—your Creation Energy—embarks on a journey of reincarnation, traversing the realms of existence in an eternal cycle of renewal and evolution.

The recognition of this profound truth holds the key to liberation and genuine freedom for humanity.

However, the comprehension of such a concept demands a level of consciousness that is currently rare on this planet.

As a result, not all individuals will be able to grasp the significance of this revelation, let alone integrate it into their worldview.

Understanding this inherent limitation deepens my appreciation for the complexities of life and fosters a sense of patience and compassion towards my fellow human beings.

I am reminded of the timeless wisdom encapsulated in the motto: "Forgive them, for they know not what they do." This mantra serves as a guiding principle, encouraging empathy and understanding in the face of human fallibility and ignorance.

Sadness vs anger

I've undergone a profound shift in how I respond to witnessing the atrocities perpetrated by my fellow Earth inhabitants.

Rather than allowing sadness to consume me, I harness the power of anger—a potent emotion that propels me towards action and drives my commitment to combatting injustice.

Whereas sadness can feel like a resignation, anger serves as a catalyst for change, igniting a fear within me to confront and address the persistence of wrongdoing.

This transformation is reflected not only in my emotional responses but also in my communication habits.

I've consciously abandoned the use of the sadness emoji and refrained from employing the word "belief," recognizing its inherent connotations of doubt and uncertainty.

Instead, I strive to cultivate a mindset grounded in clarity and conviction.

Fundamental to this shift is the understanding that the mind operates much like a computer—capable of being programmed and reprogrammed according to our intentions.

We possess the agency to take control of our mental programming, shaping our thoughts and knowledge in alignment with our values and aspirations.

Yet, this power comes with a responsibility to exercise discernment in the information we consume and the influences we allow to shape our perceptions.

In a world inundated with competing narratives and ideologies, it's imperative to remain vigilant and mindful of the content we absorb.

By taking ownership of our mental programming, we empower ourselves to navigate the complexities of existence with clarity and purpose, guided by a steadfast commitment to truth and integrity.

Brain Quotient

The Earth's population typically operates with an average Brain Quotient of around 12%.

This statistic reflects the level of cognitive development and intellectual capacity among individuals.

Reincarnation persists as a recurring cycle until one achieves a 100% Brain Quotient, signaling the culmination of the soul's evolutionary journey.

At this point, reincarnation ceases, and the individual's consciousness ascends to the esteemed High Council level, marking a profound milestone in their spiritual progression.

Our collective path forward is undeniably significant as we navigate the complexities of existence and strive to unlock the full potential of our minds.

Rather than subscribing blindly to dogma or doctrine, our focus should be on cultivating genuine understanding and insight.

Welcome to the Age of Knowledge—a time characterized by a relentless pursuit of truth and enlightenment.

Central to this journey is the imperative to learn how to think independently, free from the shackles of preconceived notions or unfounded beliefs.

It is through critical thinking and intellectual inquiry that we can transcend the limitations of ignorance and elevate our consciousness to new heights.

Let us dispel the notion of blind faith and instead embrace a mindset rooted in the relentless pursuit of knowledge.

By banishing the need to simply believe, we open ourselves to a world of boundless possibilities and profound discoveries.

Let us always strive not to merely believe but to truly know—to embark on a journey of enlightenment that transcends the confines of ignorance and leads us toward the realization of our fullest potential.

My Nose Piercings

Allow me to share a deeply personal tale that only a select few are privy to—the narrative behind why I chose to pierce my nose. In my formative years, I endured relentless mockery and ridicule due to the size of my nose, earning me the derogatory moniker "Kamion Mak" in Haitian Creole, meaning "Mack truck."

This relentless teasing fueled a desire within me to undergo a nose job, akin to the transformation pursued by the late Michael Jackson.

Hours were spent in front of the mirror, attempting to mold my nose into conformity with society's narrow standards of beauty. Yet, amidst this struggle, a profound realization dawned upon me—a realization born of introspection and self-discovery.

I began to embrace the uniqueness of my features, gradually affirming to myself the inherent beauty of my nose.

This daily ritual of self-affirmation persisted for a span of approximately three months until a pivotal moment arrived—I no longer needed to consciously remind myself of my worth.

It was during my tender teenage years, around the age of thirteen, that I unearthed the remarkable ability to deprogram and reprogram myself—a revelation that empowered me to transform perceived weaknesses into resolute strengths.

Now, I harbor a deep affection for my nose—a feature once regarded with disdain has become a symbol of empowerment and self-acceptance.

The decision to adorn it with a piercing serves as a tangible reminder of my intrinsic power and serves as an invitation for others to appreciate its unique beauty.

Such is the story behind my nose piercings—a tale imbued with profound lessons and insights.

Each narrative serves as a poignant reminder to remain attentive—to recognize the wisdom and growth inherent in every experience life bestows upon us.

THE WORD BELIEVE

I've undertaken a significant linguistic transformation by entirely removing the word "believe" from my vocabulary.

Its mere mention now triggers a physical reaction, manifesting as a headache.

This endeavor required approximately four months of concerted effort and discipline. In recognizing the mind's analogy to a sophisticated computer, with ourselves as the

primary programmers, I've seized the initiative to deprogram its inclination towards "belief" and reprogram it with the concept of "knowing."

Now, my language reflects a binary distinction: either I know, or I don't, I think, or I don't think.

The notion of belief holds no place in my worldview; I place my trust in Nothing.

From an early age, I grasped the fundamental choice between allowing external influences to shape our programming or assuming control and programming ourselves.

If one aspires to uncover the truth, the journey commences by reprogramming oneself to forsake belief in favor of a quest for knowledge.

This realization underscores the innate power we possess as individuals—the power to program and reprogram our minds according to our will.

In essence, we are all programmers, capable of wielding significant influence over our cognitive processes.

By embracing this role and exercising discernment in our programming choices, we unlock the potential for transformative personal growth and a deeper understanding of reality.

REPROGRAMMING THE MIND

The intricate process of programming or deprogramming the human mind relies heavily on the principle of repetition—an indispensable tool deeply rooted in psychological mechanisms.

This elucidates the regular attendance of individuals at their places of worship, whether it be churches, synagogues, or mosques.

These religious congregations serve as focal points for fortifying religious beliefs and nurturing faith through recurrent rituals and teachings.

As individuals engage more frequently in these religious practices, their devotion deepens, and their religious identity becomes more pronounced.

While religious adherents refer to this practice as worship, it essentially entails the systematic programming of the mind.

Repetition plays a pivotal role in embedding and reinforcing religious ideologies within the individual's consciousness.

However, what transpires when one discontinues attending these religious gatherings? A discernible shift occurs as the individual's belief in a higher power diminishes.

The waning of religious attendance diminishes the impact of religious indoctrination, gradually eroding previously held convictions.

In light of this understanding, proponents of alternative perspectives must employ a similar strategy of repetition to counteract the pervasive influence of religious programming.

By persistently reiterating the fact and incontrovertible truth that the concept of God is nonexistent, they aim to instill a contrasting worldview within the collective consciousness.

REINCARNATION

When delving into the concept of reincarnation, it's vital to dispel common misconceptions and misunderstandings that often surround this profound idea.

Contrary to popular belief, it's not the individuals themselves who undergo the process of reincarnation.

Instead, it's the Spirit form or Creation Energy that takes on a new human form with each successive lifetime.

Each incarnation brings forth a unique personality and set of circumstances yet carries with it the accumulated wisdom and knowledge of past lives.

It's crucial to grasp that the current persona one inhabits is exclusive to this particular lifetime and will not reappear in the same form again.

This underscores the belief that humans only live once, with each existence serving as a distinct chapter in the soul's journey.

While figures like Jmmanuel (Jesus Christ) and Mohammed are revered in various religious traditions, they are understood to have completed their earthly journeys and will not be seen again.

Their teachings and legacies endure, but their physical presence is finite.

However, in the case of Billy, born on February 3rd, 1937, he is the manifestation or reincarnation of the same Spiritform.

As the Prophet of the New Age, Billy offers teachings that echo those of previous prophets while expanding consciousness for both terrestrial and extraterrestrial beings.

It's worth noting that Billy is the one who imparts wisdom to the Plejaren rather than the other way around.

As the Herald of this Universe, his arrival has been anticipated for two million years, signifying a pivotal moment in cosmic evolution.

Reflecting on this profound insight and knowledge, one may begin to see individuals not merely as human beings but as embodiments of Creation Energy—each a particle of the Universal consciousness itself.

This perspective fosters a sense of interconnectedness and reverence for all life, leading to a profound appreciation for the inherent beauty within every individual.

Consequently, love becomes not just an act but an intrinsic aspect of one's being, shaping their interactions and worldview.

MOCKERY

Informing individuals that by remaining mentally subservient, they will be rewarded with heavenly riches, and praise will garner their favor and admiration.

They will eagerly place you on a pedestal, showering you with adulation and gratitude for promising such desirable outcomes.

However, it is essential to impart the deeper truth—that each individual possesses the inherent power within themselves.

Emphasize that they are their own gods, with sovereignty and autonomy resting solely within their grasp.

Remind them of their eternal nature and the concept of reincarnation, highlighting the ongoing journey of consciousness evolution.

Despite the potential for mockery and ridicule, persist in sharing this truth with sincerity and compassion.

Understand that those who react with scorn are merely entrenched in the confines of their own beliefs, unable to grasp the profound depths of self-realization and liberation.

Stay steadfast in your commitment to enlighten and empower others, for they may yet awaken from the illusions of the world and embrace the boundless potential within themselves.

IN THE HUMAN BODY

If you are within a human body, you embody an immortal light consciousness derived from the very substance of Creation.

This profound essence from which you were born ensures that you will never truly die. Your core identity is composed of the purest vibrations, which cannot be discarded or revoked.

Deep within you lies an unwavering truth that transcends all doubt: your existence is a reflection of Creation itself.

The question of why you were individuated arises from this inherent truth.

It is in the nature of Creation to produce countless fragments of itself, guiding each toward unity as a master organism while preserving their individual sovereignty.

This process represents the ultimate expression of love, as life itself is a gift imbued with love.

Though Creation cannot be discovered through mere searching, by submitting to the guiding impulse of the sovereign entity within you, you will be led unerringly.

This journey will span step by step, life after life, across universes and ages, until you ultimately gaze into the eyes of Creation and recognize your oneness with it.

In this profound realization, you will also perceive the unity of the species from which you emerged.

The fragments of the one converge through a blueprint of exploration, an endless journey whose beginning is beyond time and whose end remains unforeseeable.

WORDS OF WAID

Awaken from your dormant state and reclaim your celestial birthright.

Rise to your rightful place among the gods, embracing your ascension with the full realization of your core heritage.

About Exes

When confronted with questions about your ex or when their name arises in conversation, it's crucial to refrain from speaking negatively about them.

Such behavior not only reflects poorly on your character but also perpetuates negativity and resentment.

Despite the initial urge to criticize or express disdain, it's possible to cultivate a different response.

Recognize that every interaction, whether positive or negative, holds valuable lessons for personal growth and development.

Instead of harboring resentment or anger towards your ex, which can be detrimental to your mental well-being, choose to approach the situation with gratitude.

Acknowledge the lessons learned from the relationship, appreciating how they have contributed to your growth and evolution as an individual.

While this shift in perspective may be challenging, it is entirely achievable. I have personally experienced the transformative power of embracing gratitude and forgiveness towards my exes.

Maintaining amicable relationships and expressing love towards them is a testament to the enduring nature of true love, which transcends the boundaries of past relationships.

OPINIONS OF OTHERS

The perceptions and judgments of others hold no sway over your personal growth and evolution.

You wield no power over the thoughts and opinions that others form about you. True progression lies in the realm of self-perception.

It is within the depths of your own mind where the journey towards evolution unfolds.

Your beliefs, values, and self-assessment pave the way for your development.

Everything else—the chatter of external voices—is mere background noise in comparison.

Hence, the sentiment "only God can judge me" holds weight, but in truth, the sole arbiter of your progress is yourself.

You alone possess the ability to assess and evaluate your actions, thoughts, and character.

Your internal dialogue shapes your path, guiding you toward self-awareness, growth, and, ultimately, personal evolution.

BROKEN HEART

Love, often perceived as a matter of the heart, actually finds its roots in the intricate workings of the mind.

While the heart is merely a physical organ responsible for blood circulation, love's effects are far more profound and originate within the depths of our psyche.

When relationships falter or loved ones depart, the resulting emotional distress isn't a burden borne by the heart's chambers but rather a weight carried by the psyche.

This emotional upheaval not only impacts one's mental state but also takes a toll on physical health and overall well-being.

Prolonged dwelling on memories of lost love or shattered relationships disrupts the delicate equilibrium of the psyche, tipping the scales towards negativity and imbalance.

Such prolonged distress can lead to a cascade of detrimental effects, triggering a spiral of negative thoughts and potentially even pushing one towards contemplating self- harm or suicide.

Thus, it becomes imperative to address and manage these emotional wounds promptly and effectively to safeguard both mental and physical health.

BASICALLY

In epochs long past, advanced extraterrestrial beings descended upon Earth, seeking sanctuary from the ravages of war that plagued their distant homeworld.

Despite their technological superiority, they succumbed to the allure of Earth's inhabitants, engaging in unions that contravened a universal decree, shattering cosmic taboos.

Through these forbidden liaisons, the extraterrestrial DNA, altered and manipulated, coursed through the veins of humanity, forever altering our genetic composition.

The consequence of this intermingling is stark: humans now endure but a fraction of their intended lifespan, a grim testament to the legacy of this original transgression—an act etched in history as the original sin.

Yet, amidst this cosmic upheaval, Nokodemion, the progenitor of these errant beings, emerges as a harbinger of reconciliation.

Serving as a bridge between the flawed descendants and the enlightened Plejaren, Nokodemion endeavors to rectify the errors of the past.

The pathway to redemption unfolds through the teachings of Creation Energy, imparted by Prophet Billy.

These profound truths possess the transformative power to quell the turbulence within the human consciousness, fostering inner tranquility and awakening dormant humanity buried beneath layers of aggression.

However, the journey towards enlightenment is arduous, spanning multiple cycles of reincarnation.

Only after traversing the intricate labyrinth of existence for countless lifetimes will most Earth humans begin to grasp the profundity of these teachings.

In essence, this epoch serves as a mere seeding of the fertile soil of human consciousness, heralding the dawn of a new era—a time when the seeds of truth shall germinate, blossoming into the radiant flora of enlightenment.

THE HARSH REALITY

Welcome to the harsh realities of our world—a message of enlightenment for individuals with Black and Brown skin and a revelation of knowledge for those of White descent.

What if I were to unveil to you the stark truth that our planet harbors within its midst a multitude of barbaric and murderous beings? Initially, you may recoil in disbelief, yet the undeniable reality is this: every inhabitant of Earth, irrespective of race or creed, possesses the capacity for violence and bloodshed, capable of unleashing chaos and destruction at a moment's notice.

Retaliation, conflict, warfare, and a litany of other violent behaviors underscore the innate savagery that permeates our collective existence.

But let me be unequivocal—it is not our fault. Our genetic makeup has been tampered with by a higher race, sculpting us into instruments of warfare and carnage.

The shattered remnants of the asteroid belt stand as a haunting testament to our destructive tendencies, a stark reminder of the cataclysmic wars that once ravaged our celestial neighbors, planet Malona.

Our DNA, ingrained with an insatiable thirst for bloodshed, perpetuates a cycle of violence and oppression that plagues our world.

For individuals of Black and Brown descent, navigating a world rife with systemic racism and oppression presents a perilous challenge.

Encounters with law enforcement, regardless of the officer's skin color, carry a heightened risk of lethal consequences. In such encounters, survival hinges upon a delicate balance of compliance and deference.

To persist in the belief of equality and shared humanity with White counterparts is to court danger and risk untimely demise.

Accepting the harsh realities of our existence is paramount for self-preservation. When confronted by armed individuals with the license to kill, diplomacy and restraint may be the only means of survival.

Yet, amidst the bleakness of our reality, there exists a beacon of hope—the Creation Energy Teachings imparted by Prophet Billy.

These teachings offer a pathway to reverse the insidious manipulations of our DNA, leading us toward a harmonious alignment with the laws of Creation.

Life, in its myriad complexities and contradictions, remains a precious gift—an affirmation of love and vitality in a world steeped in darkness.

It is incumbent upon us to safeguard this precious gift by any means necessary, embracing the teachings of Prophet Billy as a guiding light toward a more enlightened and compassionate existence.

RELIGION VS CREATION ENERGY TEACHINGS

Religion, with its myriad doctrines and dogmas, often breeds a sense of existential angst, leaving adherents grappling with the uncertainties of an afterlife shrouded in mystery.

The looming specter of divine judgment and the fear of eternal consequences hang like a sword of Damocles over every decision, creating a perpetual state of apprehension and unease.

Living under the constant threat of divine retribution stifles authenticity, compelling individuals to conceal their true selves behind a veneer of conformity.

As a result, genuine connections between people become increasingly elusive, leaving each person masked and estranged, perpetuating a collective sense of alienation and disconnection.

In stark contrast, the Creation Energy Teachings, imparted by Prophet Billy, illuminate a path of clarity and inner peace.

Through these teachings, I have not only unlocked the immense power of thoughts but have also gained insight into the nature of existence beyond physical life.

With the wisdom bestowed by the Creation Energy Teachings, I understand that my journey extends far beyond the confines of this mortal coil.

Upon death, my earthly persona will dissolve, and the wisdom and knowledge accumulated in this lifetime will be seamlessly integrated into my Creation Energy, enhancing its potency and vibrancy.

From this transformative energy, a new material consciousness will emerge, guided by the preprogrammed path crafted by Creation.

Armed with this profound understanding, I embrace life fearlessly, free from the shackles of uncertainty and apprehension.

By living authentically and transparently, I invite others to truly see and understand me for who I am, fostering genuine connections and meaningful relationships based on mutual respect and understanding.

In the light of this profound wisdom, the shadows of fear dissipate, leaving behind a luminous beacon of self-assurance and inner peace.

FOLLOWER OF BILLY

To those who perceive me as merely a follower of Billy, allow me to pose a question:

Do you think that humans are born with innate mastery of every subject without the need for guidance or instruction?

Consider the disciplines of reading, writing, mathematics, English, science, history, and physical education, among others.

We all recognize that acquiring proficiency in these areas requires the guidance of teachers. Indeed, each of us has traversed the corridors of education, guided by mentors who imparted knowledge and wisdom.

So, why should I be exempt from seeking guidance while striving to remain authentic to myself?

Just as you pursued knowledge under the tutelage of educators, I, too, have sought enlightenment through the teachings of Billy.

In my case, the subject of study happens to be the Universal and Creation Truths elucidated by the Prophet Billy.

Having mastered myself, I remain an autonomous individual, much like you are after completing a course in school.

I am not a mere follower of Billy. Rather, I have assimilated the teachings he offers, recognizing him as the conduit for the Universal Truths that permeate the cosmos.

Billy serves as the harbinger of these profound insights, capable of imparting advanced Creation Teachings even to the enlightened Plejaren beings.

Just as the Plejaren do not follow Billy but rather embrace the teachings of Creation Energy, so too do I align myself with the Universal Truths unveiled through his guidance.

BILLY MEIER

Billy Meier's compassion for humanity is profound, yet he reveres our autonomy and free will. Preferring to operate from the shadows, he grants individuals the freedom to choose whether to embrace his teachings.

He shuns the trappings of fame and fortune, embodying humility in every aspect of his being. Even in personal interactions, he approaches others with genuine equality, emanating a boundless love that transcends barriers.

From the far reaches of the cosmos, seekers journey to him, drawn by the depths of his understanding of Universal Truth, a wisdom unlocked only through the Nokodemion Creation Energy.

While his influence may yet be confined to a select few, I am committed to disseminating his teachings far and wide.

My life's purpose is dedicated to this noble mission. If granted a final opportunity to address the world, I would proclaim:

"Billy Meier stands as the Prophet of the New Age.

Earthlings, heed his teachings of the Aquarian Age, for they hold the key to alleviating your burdens and ushering in a new era of enlightenment."

THE HUMAN BEING AND THE EGO

At the core of human existence resides the ego—an intricate tapestry woven from our thoughts, emotions, and perceptions, shaping our identity and defining our individuality.

When urged to suppress the ego, it's akin to asking to deny the essence of the being, to relinquish the very essence of who I am.

Accusations of possessing a sizable ego serve as a validation of my authenticity, affirming that I have presented myself unabashedly, in alignment with my true nature.

I refuse to stifle my ego, recognizing that material consciousness, personality, and ego are synonymous facets of the human experience.

I steadfastly refuse to compromise my authenticity to assuage the ignorance of others, for to do so would perpetuate a cycle of ignorance and self-denial.

Embracing the freedom inherent within my ego, I affirm my right to exist authentically, unencumbered by societal expectations or external judgments.

The Teachings of Billy

Every word uttered by Billy holds a profound truth, resonating deeply with my own lived experiences and echoing the teachings encapsulated in his books.

Inspired by the authenticity and wisdom imbued within his words, I've chosen to exemplify these teachings through my own life, not out of a desire for recognition but as a testament to their transformative power.

I swear upon my Creation Energy that every aspect of my journey mirrors the timeless wisdom conveyed in the Teachings, often to such an extent that I find myself astounded by the uncanny parallels.

My intentions are pure, driven by a genuine desire to embody the principles of peace, harmony, and spiritual growth espoused by the prophet.

Despite my earnest endeavors, I find myself confronted by misunderstanding and hostility from those who fail to grasp the depth of these teachings.

Yet, I harbor no ill will, extending an olive branch in the hope that others may also embrace the path of enlightenment and compassion.

This choice to embody the teachings was made with full awareness of the challenges it would entail.

While some opt to hoard their knowledge to avoid such tribulations, I stand resolute, prepared to confront whatever obstacles may come my way.

In the face of adversity, I remain steadfast in my commitment to fostering understanding and empathy.

I implore others to take a moment to perceive me not as an adversary but as a fellow traveler on the path toward enlightenment, striving to create a world infused with peace, harmony, and mutual respect.

Beyond Death

Beyond death, the essence of "Waid" transcends the confines of individual identity, serving merely as the vessel for a unique personality in this current lifetime.

However, upon the cessation of physical existence, this persona dissipates, destined never to resurface again.

Yet, the energy that once animated this persona undergoes a profound transformation as it merges with the cosmic fabric of Creation, undergoing a process of reprogramming and renewal.

From this crucible emerges a new material consciousness, a fresh iteration of personality and ego, poised to embark on a new journey of existence.

In this cycle of reincarnation, the accumulated wisdom and knowledge gleaned from countless past lives become accessible to the emerging consciousness.

This wealth of experience and insight serves as a reservoir of guidance and understanding, ready to be tapped into by the nascent individual once they become aware of their existence.

Thus, while the persona of "Waid" fades into oblivion, the eternal essence that underlies it persists, perpetuating the continuum of existence across lifetimes and epochs.

In this perpetual cycle of renewal and rebirth, the journey of self-discovery and evolution unfolds, guided by the enduring legacy of past experiences and the boundless potential of the future.

THE **OCB** - OVERALL CONSCIOUSNESS BLOCK

Being in constant connection with the Overall Consciousness Block (OCB) is akin to effortlessly navigating an autonomous car.

In this state, the burdens of decision-making and control dissipate as you trust implicitly in the guidance and support of a higher power within.

Every choice, decision, action, behavior, and reaction flow seamlessly in alignment with the laws and recommendations of Creation.

With this profound sense of alignment, you exude an unwavering confidence that every step you take is imbued with purpose and wisdom.

In this state of deep connection, fear and worry become distant echoes, overshadowed by an abiding sense of tranquility and assurance.

Despite the chaos and discord that may swirl around you, you remain anchored in the certainty that all is unfolding as it should, guided by the benevolent forces of the Universe.

Through this profound connection, you tap into the limitless power of your thoughts, recognizing their profound influence in shaping your reality.

With clarity and conviction, you navigate the currents of existence with grace and ease, secure in the knowledge that you are held and supported by the boundless expanse of the cosmos.

You Are Your Words

At the core of human existence lies the profound connection between individuals and their words.

Words serve as the vehicle through which humans articulate their thoughts, emotions, and experiences, much like how communication systems function within the animal kingdom and across the vast expanse of nature.

Just as various species convey messages and meanings through their unique language systems, humans harness the power of language to communicate, connect, and interact with one another.

It is through the mastery of language that individuals unlock the full potential of their words, imbuing them with transformative power and influence.

When wielded with skill and intentionality, words possess the capacity to resonate deeply with others, evoking emotions, inspiring action, and fostering understanding.

Through the artful expression of thoughts and ideas, individuals can captivate audiences, provoke reflection, and effect meaningful change in the world around them.

Indeed, the potency of one's words lies not merely in their utterance but in the conviction, clarity, and authenticity with which they are delivered.

By honing their linguistic prowess and cultivating a deep understanding of the impact of their words, individuals can harness the full extent of their communicative abilities, compelling others to listen, engage, and respond.

THE DEATH PENALTY

The inherent flaws and moral contradictions of the death penalty transcend mere legal or ethical debates.

No individual, regardless of their actions or transgressions, should be condemned to death as a means of illustrating the immorality of killing.

Such rationale, rooted in the desire for retribution, fails to uphold the sanctity of life and perpetuates a cycle of violence.

The antiquated notion of "an eye for an eye" is not only archaic but also antithetical to the principles of Creation, which emphasize compassion, redemption, and the inherent worth of every individual.

Each person, irrespective of their past deeds, deserves the opportunity to pursue personal growth, seek redemption, and learn from their mistakes.

The continued practice of the death penalty in any society undermines the very foundation of civilization. It reflects a regression to primitive forms of justice rooted in vengeance and cruelty rather than progress and enlightenment.

A society that sanctions such barbaric punishments cannot lay claim to true civility or moral superiority.

By abolishing the death penalty and embracing more humane forms of justice, societies can affirm their commitment to the principles of compassion, rehabilitation, and respect for human dignity.

Only through the recognition of the inherent worth and potential for redemption in every individual can we truly aspire towards a more just and enlightened civilization.

Politics

My evolution from identifying as a liberal to questioning the fundamental tenets of the political spectrum has been a profound journey of disillusionment and revelation.

Initially drawn to liberal ideologies by the promise of freedom and autonomy, my disillusionment began with the Covid vaccination debacle, where liberals, purported champions of personal autonomy, demonstrated a blatant disregard for individual rights by advocating for mandatory vaccinations.

My aversion to wars, a core liberal principle, was shattered when I witnessed the hypocrisy within the liberal establishment. Despite their professed stance against war, the liberal leadership, exemplified by figures like Biden, revealed their complicity in perpetuating conflict.

Biden's unabashed support for Zionism and the atrocities inflicted upon Palestinians under the guise of party politics unveiled the hypocrisy at the heart of liberal warmongering.

As I observed the disturbing escalation of conflicts, from the suppression of peaceful protests to the insidious funding of wars in regions like Ukraine, I realized the perilous trajectory orchestrated by the liberal elite.

The reckless pursuit of geopolitical agendas, fueled by misguided interventions and military escalation, posed a far greater threat to global stability than the prospect of electing a contentious figure lacking political finesse.

While the choice between political ideologies may seem stark, the underlying reality transcends partisan divides.

In confronting the existential threats posed by war and nuclear escalation, my perspective shifted from ideological allegiance to a pragmatic assessment of the prevailing dangers.

Sacrificing a country to preserve the integrity of the planet may appear drastic, yet it underscores the imperative of prioritizing collective survival over political allegiances.

In embracing the stark realities of our geopolitical landscape, my allegiance to political ideologies gave way to a commitment to truth and logic.

The recognition of systemic dysfunction and moral bankruptcy within both liberal and conservative spheres compelled me to reassess my political identity as a neutral, non, politically affiliated human being, guided by a steadfast commitment to reason and humanity's collective welfare.

TWIN FLAMES

Life has a peculiar way of juxtaposing individuals, transforming strangers encountered on a bus into the cherished love of one's life in subsequent chapters.

Contrary to the romanticized notions of soul mates or twin flames, this phenomenon is not predetermined by some cosmic design but rather emerges from the intricate interplay of chance, choice, and circumstance.

The concept of soul mates or twin flames, while appealing, is ultimately a construct born from the depths of human longing and desire for connection.

It reflects humanity's innate yearning for a sense of belonging and profound companionship, projecting idealized fantasies onto the enigmatic realm of relationships.

Yet, the truth is far more nuanced and complex. The connections we forge with others are multifaceted and dynamic, shaped by a myriad of factors ranging from shared interests and values to serendipitous encounters and mutual growth.

Rather than subscribing to the notion of predetermined soul mates, it's far more empowering to embrace the fluidity and unpredictability of human relationships, recognizing that love and connection can manifest in myriad forms and iterations throughout our lives.

THE BELIEVER

The believer perceives themselves through the lens of perpetual childhood, viewing personal growth and evolution as unattainable aspirations.

This perspective is rooted in their self-identification as children of God, a notion that permeates their worldview and shapes their relationship with spirituality.

In their paradigm, believers entrust the interpretation of divine wisdom to authoritative figures, compensating them to recite the words of God.

This reliance stems from a perceived incapacity to engage with religious texts independently, akin to the illiteracy of a child unable to decipher written language or formulate independent thoughts.

Consequently, believers perceive themselves as bereft of agency, ill-equipped to navigate life's complexities without external guidance. Thus, they attribute all glory and significance to God, relegating their own existence to a state of insignificance and dependency.

This self-effacing stance poses a fundamental paradox: how can one acknowledge the worth and dignity of others when they fail to recognize their own intrinsic value?

Paradoxically, these same individuals espouse beliefs in divine benevolence while imposing adult responsibilities on their own offspring as soon as they reach legal maturity.

The disparity between their expectations for themselves and their children underscores their dependency on an imagined paternal figure in the heavens.

WORDS OF WAID

This reliance extends to the belief in a divine savior who absolves them of personal accountability, shielding them from the burdens of self-reflection and introspection.

By perpetuating the illusion of perpetual childhood, believers evade the inherent responsibilities of adulthood, shirking accountability for their actions and choices.

Perhaps it's time for them to relinquish the security blanket of spiritual infancy and embrace the challenges and privileges of maturity, forsaking the allure of rebirth in favor of genuine personal growth.

THE TAPESTRY OF LIFE

In the grand tapestry of life, the external trappings hold little significance.

Whether one resides in opulent splendor, cruising in the latest luxury vehicle soaring through the skies in a private jet, or inhabits a modest one-bedroom abode while relying on public transportation, the essence of existence transcends material possessions.

What truly matters is the intrinsic joy derived from the act of living itself. It's imperative to internalize the notion that life is a series of lessons, each unique in its demands and complexities, necessitating varied lifestyles to navigate them effectively.

It's essential to recognize that one's circumstances do not define their worth or purpose.

You may not find yourself occupying the throne of a monarch, gracing the covers of magazines as a renowned artist, grappling with addiction, or grappling with the burden of a murderous past simply because those were not the lessons ordained for you in this lifetime. Instead of harboring envy towards those whose paths diverge from our own, it's far more constructive to champion everyone's endeavors to succeed in their individual journeys of growth and self-discovery.

By fostering a culture of mutual support and encouragement, we collectively contribute to the enrichment of each other's lives, embracing the diverse lessons that shape our shared human experience.

TRUE SELF

The tendency to become ensnared by the opinions of others often leads individuals to self-imposed captivity.

Despite earnest efforts, many fail to grasp the fundamental truth that they wield no dominion over how others perceive them.

Regardless of the meticulously crafted facade one presents to the world, individuals will inevitably form their own judgments, colored by their unique perspectives and biases.

In light of this immutable reality, the most prudent course of action is to remain authentic to oneself.

However, a disconcerting number of individuals opt to conform to societal norms, laboring under the misguided belief that everyone else is following suit.

Yet, this assumption is fallacious. In truth, a multitude of people are bravely embracing their true selves, unfettered by the shackles of conformity.

It is our interpretation that errs, as we misread their genuine authenticity, blinded by our preconceived notions and societal expectations.

THE WORD BELIEVE

The word "believe" has become increasingly cumbersome for me to employ when articulating my sentiments.

Its mere utterance seems to trigger a throbbing headache within me. It has dawned on me that humans should grasp the intricacies of how their power is harnessed.

It begins with doubt, emanating from the depths of one's subconsciousness. Consequently, words born from doubt carry the same weight, resulting in a dilution of their potency.

Your power lies within your words. When these words are rooted in beliefs, they lack the vigor to effectuate change.

Conversely, words grounded in knowledge and truth possess an inherent dynamism.

This potency reverberates, resonating with everyone in its path.

The formidable force of truth is unmistakable, transcending boundaries and leaving an indelible impact.

Hence, I advocate for relinquishing belief in favor of embracing knowledge. This includes disavowing blind faith in oneself.

Instead, endeavor to comprehend the depths of your being. Only through self-awareness and a pursuit of truth can one wield true power and influence.

Your Children

As your children transition into adulthood, it's imperative to grant them the autonomy to chart their own course in life.

Your influence on their decisions dwindles as they assume greater responsibility for their choices.

Your primary duty shifts towards providing unwavering support, demonstrating love, and extending guidance only when solicited.

While they may have come into existence through you, it's essential to acknowledge that they are not possessions to be controlled.

Rather, they are autonomous entities embarking on their unique journey of self- discovery, poised to encounter triumphs, setbacks, and pivotal moments of growth.

By affording them the liberty to navigate life's intricacies on their terms, you facilitate opportunities for them to learn from firsthand experiences.

This act of empowering them to glean insights from their own triumphs and tribulations embodies the essence of genuine love — a love that transcends ownership and fosters personal development and self-realization.

BILLY

Billy Meier is an enigmatic and captivating individual whose narrative is steeped in mystique.

Central to his story is the presence of an entity known as Nokodemion, who, having traversed an extensive existence within the semi-material realm of the High Council, achieved the remarkable feat of attaining the Arahat Athersata level in his spiritual form or Creation Energy (CE).

This CE, boasting a staggering age of 9.6 billion years, has been bestowed with a profound mission according to the laws of Creation.

As per these laws, when the inaugural human or spiritual entity (CE) ascends to the initial purely spiritual tier within a universe, they are entrusted with disseminating knowledge pertaining to Spiritual and Creational laws among the denizens of said universe.

Across epochs, Nokodemion has undergone numerous incarnations on Earth, assuming roles ranging from prophets to influential figures who have indelibly shaped human cognition.

These incarnations encompass illustrious personalities such as Galileo, Socrates, Aristotle, Felix Mendelssohn, Mozart, Rasputin, and others. Notably, several of Nokodemion's reincarnations are referenced in the Bible, including Henoch, Jeremiah, Isaiah, Elijah, Jmmanuel (also known as Jesus), and Mohammed.

Presently, the spirit of Nokodemion inhabits the vessel of Billy Meier, heralded as the Prophet of the New Age.

It's pertinent to clarify that the term "Prophet" here connotes a harbinger of truth and is divorced from any religious connotations.

WORDS OF WAID

Billy Meier's incarnation marks the seventh and final iteration of Nokodemion as a prophet.

Following Billy's eventual demise, a reincarnation is anticipated around the year 2075 to perpetuate the Spiritual Teachings.

This forthcoming reincarnation will be distinguishable by a birthmark located where Jmmanuel (Jesus Christ) was pierced during the crucifixion.

Nokodemion is slated to remain on Earth until the year 3999, thereafter returning to the spiritual realms of Arahat Athersata to pursue its own evolutionary journey.

ADULTHOOD AND NEW LIFE

When a baby transitions into adolescence, we don't mourn the loss of their infancy, recognizing it as a natural progression in life's journey.

Similarly, we comprehend that aging and, ultimately, death are intrinsic facets of existence.

Death, much like the transition from infancy to adulthood, signifies the evolution of life into a new form, with a unique identity inhabiting a fresh human vessel. It's essential for individuals to grasp that death isn't a cessation of life but rather a continuation of its eternal essence.

The perpetuity of life extends beyond physical boundaries, encompassing wisdom, knowledge, and love.

Death and birth are intertwined, serving as complementary aspects of the same existence, symbolizing the duality inherent in life's continuum.

Different Opinions

Even in the present day, a notable number of acquaintances and family members maintain a rift in communication due to conflicting stances on political views.

This divergence in viewpoints appears to fuel a reluctance to reconcile despite the fundamental value of diversity in perspectives, which enriches our collective experience.

It seems irrational that individuals would opt for estrangement over embracing the mosaic of opinions that define us.

Embracing the ethos of agreeing to disagree and moving forward is imperative.

While it's not obligatory to endorse divergent views, it is essential to uphold the autonomy of individuals to hold their own beliefs.

Respect for differing opinions, even in the absence of personal agreement, is crucial for nurturing harmony and fostering peace among people.

Show Love Now

Don't wait until our loved ones pass away to express our affection and appreciation for them. Instead, let's take action while they are still with us.

Once someone has passed on, all avenues of communication are closed. No matter how loudly we may cry out, they cannot hear us.

Regardless of the depth of our sorrow, they cannot feel our pain.

They won't be able to witness our regret for not reaching out sooner because they will no longer be here.

Therefore, it's essential to demonstrate love and care for each other while we're still alive and present in this world together.

This proactive approach fosters peace and harmony among us.

Unlearn

Earth humans must come to a profound realization: we need to let go of everything we have always believed to be true.

The entirety of our knowledge and understanding is built on beliefs, many of which are fundamentally flawed or untrue.

This recognition is crucial because our beliefs are often based on limited perceptions, cultural biases, and misinformation.

To truly advance and grow, humans must engage in a rigorous process of unlearning. This means critically examining and dismantling the assumptions and misconceptions that have shaped our worldview.

It requires a willingness to question long-held notions and to recognize the limitations of our current understanding.

Once humans have cleared away these outdated beliefs, we can embark on the path of learning anew.

This new learning involves seeking knowledge with an open mind, embracing uncertainty, and valuing evidence and reason over preconceived ideas. It is a continuous process of growth and adaptation, where every new piece of information is weighed and considered within a broader, more nuanced perspective.

The journey ahead for Earth humans is one of profound transformation. We must unlearn what we think we know and be open to learning from a place of genuine curiosity and humility.

This involves shedding the false security provided by outdated beliefs and embracing a mindset that welcomes change and new insights.

By doing so, we can uncover deeper truths and achieve a more enlightened state of understanding.

This transformative process is not just about accumulating knowledge but about fostering a more sophisticated, adaptable, and inclusive way of thinking.

It allows us to break free from the confines of narrow perspectives and to appreciate the complexity and interconnectedness of the universe.

This journey of unlearning and relearning is essential for our collective evolution.

It enables us to create a more just, compassionate, and enlightened world where we can address the challenges we face with wisdom and foresight.

Only through this process can we hope to realize our true potential and contribute meaningfully to the future of humanity.

Badge of Honor

Many people extol God as a badge of honor, displaying their faith as a mark of virtue. However, I perceive a more troubling aspect behind this display.

These individuals often harbor a profound fear of life itself, perceiving themselves as too weak, meaningless, and insignificant to navigate existence independently.

Their deep-seated anxieties lead them to cling ever more tightly to their faith in a divine figure.

The greater their fear, the more fervently they embrace their beliefs, using them as a shield to soothe their insecurities and find a sense of security in an unpredictable world.

This brings us to a profound question: How would you live your life if you knew you were eternal and that, truly, there was absolutely nothing to fear but fear itself?

Imagine embracing the understanding that your existence transcends the physical realm and that your essence is eternal.

How would this knowledge transform your approach to life's challenges and uncertainties?

Would you still seek validation through external symbols of faith, or would you find strength within yourself? Would you approach life with greater courage, embracing each moment with confidence and curiosity, knowing that every experience is a part of an endless journey?

Acknowledging your eternal nature could liberate you from the chains of fear, empowering you to live more fully and authentically.

Instead of seeking refuge in faith driven by fear, you could cultivate a profound sense of inner peace and resilience.

Embracing the concept of your own eternal essence encourages a deeper understanding of life's true nature, fostering a mindset where fear is not a dominant force but a transient emotion to be acknowledged and transcended.

This shift in perspective could lead to a more enriched and liberated existence, allowing you to navigate life with grace and unwavering confidence.

OPINIONS

Earth humans often place great importance on their own viewpoints and opinions, frequently interpreting any form of disagreement as an act of hostility.

In doing so, they overlook a fundamental truth: resistance is an indispensable catalyst for growth and progress. If everyone always agreed with you, there would be no evolution.

Despite this, people are often willing to discard valuable relationships over differences in opinion, disregarding the fact that these very differences are essential for their own evolution.

This behavior typically occurs when an individual has not mastered self-control and self-awareness. The ego, or material consciousness, feels it is of utmost importance and believes it knows better, thus placing itself above fellow human beings in intelligence.

This mindset prevents individuals from understanding that we are all students and teachers, equal in value.

The true measure of wisdom lies in recognizing the equal worth of others and the importance of diverse perspectives for mutual growth.

In essence, the inability to accept and learn from differing opinions is a sign of an underdeveloped sense of self and an overinflated ego.

It highlights the ongoing journey Earth humans must undertake to achieve greater self- mastery and mutual respect.

Recognizing and embracing this dynamic can lead to healthier relationships and a more evolved society.

THE TEACHINGS

The world we know is destined to undergo profound transformation through the teachings of Nokodemion, the oldest Creation Energy of the entire Universe.

As Earth's inhabitants reconnect with these ancient teachings, they will gradually shed their aggressive tendencies, evolving into true human beings and leaving behind their barbaric traits.

Nokodemion, the first human being to attain the pure Spirit level of Arahat Athersata, continues to influence and guide us through Billy, the Prophet of the New Age.

This sacred wisdom lives on within him, offering us a path toward enlightenment and a higher state of being.

Embracing Nokodemion's teachings means acknowledging a reality where we strive for inner peace, understanding, and a harmonious existence with all life forms.

The sooner we accept and integrate these teachings into our lives, the quicker we can catalyze a collective shift toward a more enlightened and compassionate world.

This transformation is not just a hopeful vision but a necessary evolution for humanity. It calls for a deep and sincere commitment to personal growth and spiritual development, recognizing the interconnectedness of all beings and the universe.

By embracing this path, we can transcend our current limitations and contribute to the creation of a more just, peaceful, and enlightened global community.

Life's Approach

Approach life with a growth mindset and embrace every experience with gratitude, whether they brings joy or challenges.

Recognize that every encounter, regardless of its nature, offers an opportunity for growth and learning.

Be thankful to those who help us, acknowledging their positive impact on our lives. Equally, extend gratitude to those who hurt us.

This practice helps release any resentment or bitterness, facilitating healing and enabling us to move forward with a lighter heart.

Adopting this mindset also cultivates empathy, understanding, and a deeper appreciation for life's complexities. It encourages us to see beyond the immediate pain or pleasure, recognizing the valuable lessons embedded in each experience.

By remembering that "it's all lessons," we can navigate life's ups and downs with grace, resilience, and a heart full of gratitude.

This perspective transforms obstacles into opportunities for personal growth and fosters a resilient spirit capable of enduring and thriving through life's myriad challenges.

SEEING DEAD LOVED ONES AGAIN

When considering reunions with deceased loved ones in the spiritual realm, have you pondered the physical aspects of such encounters? Will they appear healthy, whole, and vibrant, regardless of their physical condition at the time of passing? Will they be clothed or unclothed? How will you locate them amidst the vast multitude? Are there designated meeting points or welcoming gates for families?

These questions highlight the complexities of conceptualizing such reunions.

The idea of seeing loved ones again in an afterlife, complete with physical attributes and familiar surroundings, can often seem like wishful thinking.

It may not align with logical or realistic perspectives.

Instead, we need to realize that loved ones continue to exist within us as memories— eternal and cherished.

Love itself is eternal, transcending physical presence and continuing to shape our lives long after loved ones are gone.

Embracing this reality can be a beautiful and liberating experience. It allows us to find comfort and meaning in the enduring impact of those we have lost.

By focusing on the present, we can find beauty in the here and now.

Accepting that loved ones who have passed on are no longer physically present can help us appreciate the depth of our memories and the ways in which they influence our current lives.

The concept of reincarnation suggests that they may return as new beings with new personalities. When you encounter them again in a

125

future life, the love you once shared may be felt anew by both of you, albeit in different forms.

This understanding encourages us to cherish the present moment and the connections we have now rather than longing for reunions that may be rooted in illusion.

It teaches us to appreciate the eternal nature of love and the ways in which it continues to shape our existence.

CRITICAL THINKING

As a child, I was indoctrinated and brainwashed through movies, cartoons, and books to believe that Native Americans were the savages while the white cowboys were the virtuous heroes.

This narrative was pervasive in the media and education I consumed, painting a black- and-white picture of good versus evil.

However, as I grew older and began to educate myself, I discovered that this depiction was a gross distortion of reality.

In fact, it was often the cowboys and settlers who committed acts of violence and displacement against Indigenous peoples.

The stories I had been told were part of a larger pattern of misinformation and propaganda designed to justify historical injustices.

If this sounds familiar, it's because similar tactics are being used today in various conflicts around the world, including the situation between Israel and the Palestinian people.

Manipulative narratives are still crafted to shape public perception, often obscuring the true nature of the conflict and the suffering of those involved.

We must remain vigilant and critical of the stories we are told. Misinformation and propaganda can shape our perceptions just as effectively now as they did in the past.

The world is often well aware of who truly perpetrates acts of evil and genocide, even though those committing these atrocities seek to mask their actions with false narratives.

WORDS OF WAID

As Vladimir Putin himself said, there's no point in trying to compete against the West's propaganda machine—you will get crushed.

Despite this, we must not be swayed by their lies. Seeking the truth and questioning the information presented to us is crucial.

This practice is known as critical thinking.

It involves analyzing and evaluating the information we encounter, questioning its sources and intentions, and striving to understand the broader context.

By honing our critical thinking skills, we can navigate through the noise and deception, uncovering the realities that are often hidden from plain view.

In a world where narratives can be manipulated, and facts can be twisted, critical thinking is our strongest tool for uncovering the truth and fostering a more just and informed society.

THE TRUTH

The truth cannot stay concealed forever. Over time, it emerges and becomes undeniable, even to those who are the most skeptical.

Regardless of the effort put into hiding it, the truth has an intrinsic nature that compels it to surface and reveal itself.

In time, the clarity and evidence supporting the truth become so overwhelming that even the most doubtful individuals are forced to acknowledge its existence.

It's a process that might be slow and arduous, but eventually, the undeniable force of reality breaks through the barriers of deception and denial.

Therefore, let the truth be your guiding light. In its illumination lies the real and true peace.

By embracing and upholding the truth, you cultivate an inner tranquility that falsehoods can never provide.

Living in harmony with the truth fosters a sense of authenticity and integrity, allowing you to navigate life with confidence and clarity.

In the presence of truth, all facades fall away, and what remains is a genuine peace that endures.

This peace is not just an absence of conflict but a profound alignment with reality that nurtures the soul and fosters genuine connections with others.

So, seek the truth, cherish it, and let it guide your path, for therein lies the essence of true peace and fulfillment.

TRUST IN YOURSELF

You possess an incredible strength and resilience that empower you to overcome any challenges that come your way.

No matter how difficult or overwhelming a situation may seem, you have an abundance of inner resources and abilities to handle it effectively.

Life will never present you with obstacles that are beyond your capacity to manage.

Trust in your capability to navigate through tough times, for you are equipped with the fortitude and wisdom necessary to endure and triumph over adversity.

It's essential to recognize and embrace your own potential.

By understanding yourself and tapping into your full power, you can face any challenge head-on and emerge victorious.

Trust in your strength, rely on your resilience, and know that you have what it takes to succeed.

RESENTMENT

Let go of resentment, as holding onto it can significantly harm your health.

Resentment cultivates feelings of anger, bitterness, and tension, which can elevate stress levels and lead to a range of physical ailments.

These negative emotions can manifest in various ways, such as headaches, high blood pressure, and a weakened immune system, ultimately compromising your overall physical health.

Moreover, harboring resentment disrupts your mental peace. It keeps your mind in a constant state of turmoil, making it difficult to find tranquility and focus.

This mental unrest can spill over into your relationships, creating conflict and disharmony with those around you.

The persistent negativity can strain interactions with loved ones, friends, and colleagues, further impacting your emotional well-being.

By gradually releasing these negative emotions, you allow yourself to experience a profound sense of relief and emotional freedom.

Letting go of resentment helps to clear your mind and restore inner peace, making way for positive thoughts and feelings.

This process can lead to improved mental clarity, reduced stress, and a more positive outlook on life.

The more you practice letting go, the more noticeable the improvements in your overall well-being will be.

Mentally, you will find it easier to cope with daily challenges and maintain a balanced state of mind.

Physically, you may experience fewer stress-related ailments and a greater sense of vitality.

Embracing forgiveness and moving forward can lead to a more harmonious and fulfilling life.

Forgiveness allows you to release the hold that past grievances have on you, paving the way for healthier relationships and a more positive and contented existence.

By letting go of resentment and practicing forgiveness, you open the door to a more peaceful, joyful, and enriched life.

THE TRAIN OF LIFE

Imagine that life is like being on a train. We're all passengers, each with the freedom to move from one car to another or stay comfortable in our chosen seats.

This journey represents our experiences, choices, and opportunities.

We interact with fellow travelers, make decisions about where we want to be, and sometimes change our paths along the way.

Despite our movements and decisions within the train, its journey continues on a predetermined route.

The train symbolizes the inevitability of time and the progression of our lives. No matter how we choose to spend our time on the train, it will eventually reach each scheduled stop.

These stops represent the milestones and phases we encounter throughout our lives.

Some passengers may find that reaching their destination takes longer than anticipated. This delay can be due to various personal circumstances, choices, or unforeseen events.

However, the train's unwavering progress ensures that everyone will eventually arrive at their intended stop, symbolizing the certainty of the Creation course.

In essence, the journey on the train reminds us that while we have the freedom to make choices and shape our experiences, certain aspects of life remain beyond our control.

The train will reach its stops just as time and life will continue to move forward.

WORDS OF WAID

Embracing this journey allows us to find a balance between exercising our freedom and accepting the inevitabilities of life's progression.

KNOWING AND NOT KNOWING

It's important to move away from the mindset of professing ignorance and being content with it.

Acknowledging a lack of knowledge is a vital first step, but it should be followed by a willingness to learn and grow.

Being proud of ignorance can hinder personal development and limit opportunities.

Embracing a growth mindset, where you actively seek to expand your understanding, can lead to more fulfilling experiences and achievements.

Celebrating ignorance can create a culture where learning and intellectual curiosity are undervalued.

This attitude can spread to others, discouraging them from seeking knowledge and improving their skills.

Instead, fostering an environment where learning is valued, and ignorance is seen as a temporary state can encourage continuous self-improvement and collective progress.

It's crucial to understand that everyone starts somewhere, but it's the journey of learning that defines us.

Moreover, the world is constantly evolving, with new information and discoveries emerging daily.

Remaining stagnant in your knowledge base can result in being left behind in both professional and personal contexts.

Staying informed and educated is necessary to adapt to changes and seize new opportunities.

By rejecting pride in ignorance and striving for knowledge, you can better navigate the complexities of modern life and contribute meaningfully to society.

The goal should be to replace the pride in not knowing with a passion for learning.

Embrace curiosity and the pursuit of understanding as fundamental aspects of personal and communal growth.

Recognize that admitting what you don't know is not a weakness but an invitation to learn.

This shift in attitude can open doors to new possibilities, enrich your life experiences, and empower you to make more informed decisions.

INSATIABLE

Humans often find themselves perpetually unsatisfied, constantly seeking more once they have attained their desires.

This insatiable hunger drives them to always yearn for greater achievements, possessions, or experiences, revealing a fundamental aspect of human nature.

The pursuit of fulfillment seems endless, as the attainment of one goal merely leads to the setting of another.

This relentless quest can be attributed to an inherent greed that knows no bounds.

The desire for more wealth, power, and material possessions can dominate one's life, overshadowing the simple joys and contentment that could otherwise be found.

The cycle of wanting and acquiring can become a trap, preventing people from appreciating what they already have.

However, there comes a point when individuals must confront a deeper truth: material possessions and superficial gains are fleeting.

In the grand scheme of life and beyond, these are akin to monopoly coins, mere tokens for temporary play.

The true value lies not in what can be owned or accumulated but in the intangible aspects of life.

The only things that can be carried beyond this earthly existence are wisdom and knowledge.

These are the real treasures, enduring beyond the physical realm and enriching the Creation Energy of the human being.

Recognizing this truth can shift one's focus from endless accumulation to the pursuit of learning and understanding, which brings lasting fulfillment and purpose.

THINK INSTEAD OF REACTING.

When faced with a situation, our initial impulse often is to react immediately.

However, pausing to think before responding can lead to more thoughtful and effective outcomes.

This practice helps in understanding the situation better and considering various perspectives.

Instead of letting emotions drive our actions, taking a moment to reflect fosters more constructive and measured responses.

Thinking before reacting also allows us to evaluate the consequences of our actions. Immediate reactions are often based on instinct and emotion, which sometimes lead to regrettable outcomes.

By thinking things through, we can anticipate the potential impact of our response and choose a course of action that is more likely to yield positive results.

This considered approach can prevent misunderstandings and conflicts.

Moreover, a thoughtful response enhances communication and relationships.

When we take the time to process information and reflect on our responses, we demonstrate respect and consideration for others.

This thoughtful engagement builds trust and rapport, making interactions more meaningful and productive.

It shows that we value the other person's perspective and are willing to invest time in understanding their viewpoint.

THE DREAM

Before I even knew who Billy Meier was, I had a dream that was so compelling I felt the need to document it.

Back in the days of MySpace, I shared it online. The dream was so vivid it left a lasting impression on me. It went something like this: we were in a huge assembly with many different people present, and on the big screens, we were given an important message.

The message on the screens said, "We're seeking volunteers to rescue some of our loved ones who are trapped on a planet.

This is a rescue mission. In this mission, you'll relinquish your godly abilities, endure the passage of time, and you will suffer greatly.

Your task is to reactivate and awaken them from their profound slumber." This dream felt incredibly significant, and I couldn't shake the feeling that it had a deeper meaning.

It was only later, when I stumbled upon Billy Meier's teachings on YouTube, that everything began to fall into place for me.

His ideas and messages resonated deeply with the content of my dream, providing a context that I hadn't understood before. I felt a strong connection between what I had dreamt and what I was learning from Meier's teachings.

This realization was profound and transformative for me. I came to understand why I am here and what my purpose in life is.

My life is now dedicated to the mission described in my dream. I feel a sense of duty and commitment to this purpose, and it guides my actions and decisions every day.

Indeed, as the Creation Energy teachings show, cultivating the habit of thinking before reacting can significantly improve our personal and professional lives.

It allows us to respond more wisely and effectively, reducing the likelihood of negative consequences and fostering better relationships.

By prioritizing thoughtfulness over immediate reaction, we can navigate challenges with greater clarity and poise.

This approach not only benefits us but also positively impacts those around us.

Seek Knowledge

The most crucial task for a human being is to eliminate beliefs from their consciousness.

Beliefs are only based on assumptions and unverified information and limit one's understanding and perspective.

By clinging to beliefs, individuals hinder their ability to see the world as it truly is and to engage with it in a meaningful way.

Eradicating these beliefs allows for a clearer, more open-minded approach to life.

The era of living based on beliefs has reached its end. Beliefs may have provided comfort and a sense of certainty because we didn't know.

But in the New age, they create divisions and misconceptions.

The complexities of contemporary life demand more than just belief. They also require a foundation built on evidence and reason.

The time has come to move beyond the confines of belief and embrace a new paradigm centered on knowledge and understanding.

Human beings must now turn their focus toward seeking knowledge. Knowledge, unlike belief, is grounded in evidence, reason, and critical thinking.

It involves a rigorous process of inquiry and verification, which leads to a more accurate and comprehensive understanding of the world.

By prioritizing knowledge, people will be able to navigate life more effectively, making decisions based on facts rather than untested assumptions.

Through the pursuit of knowledge, a deeper comprehension of life can be achieved. Knowledge empowers individuals to question, explore, and understand the nuances of existence.

It fosters intellectual growth and the ability to adapt to new information and changing circumstances.

Only by seeking knowledge can humans hope to gain a better understanding of life and ultimately improve their individual and collective experiences.

A Lesson In Every Interaction

In every interaction we have, there's always a lesson to be learned. Each encounter, whether brief or prolonged, holds the potential to teach us something valuable.

The challenge often lies in recognizing and understanding these lessons amidst the hustle and bustle of our daily lives.

Sometimes, these lessons are clear and immediate.

For example, a friendly conversation with a colleague might offer insights into better communication techniques or new perspectives on a project.

Other times, the lessons are more subtle and require reflection to uncover, such as understanding the deeper reasons behind a disagreement with a friend.

It's up to us to actively seek out and interpret these lessons.

This requires a mindful approach to our interactions, paying close attention to both what is said and unsaid.

By doing so, we can gain a better understanding of ourselves and others, fostering personal growth and improving our relationships.

Viewing each interaction as an opportunity to learn transforms our daily experiences.

Instead of simply going through the motions, we can approach life with curiosity and openness, ready to glean wisdom from every conversation and encounter.

This mindset not only enriches our lives but also equips us with the tools to navigate the complexities of human relationships more effectively.

AUTHENTICITY

It's crucial to never let anyone pressure you into becoming someone you're not. External influences can sometimes be strong and persuasive, but maintaining your individuality is vital.

Succumbing to the demands or expectations of others can lead to a loss of your true self, which can have long-term negative effects on your well-being.

Staying true to yourself requires a strong sense of self-awareness and confidence. It means understanding who you are, what you know, and stand for.

This self-awareness forms the foundation of your authentic personality, allowing you to navigate life with integrity and honesty.

By embracing your true self, you not only respect your own identity but also set a powerful example for others.

Authenticity in personality is not just about resisting external pressures but also about embracing your own unique traits and characteristics.

Everyone has a distinct combination of strengths, weaknesses, and quirks that make them who they are.

Celebrating these differences instead of trying to conform to others' expectations is key to building a genuine and fulfilling life.

It's this authenticity that allows you to connect deeply with others and build meaningful relationships based on mutual respect and understanding.

The journey to becoming authentic to yourself involves continuous self-reflection and growth.

It means constantly checking in with yourself to ensure that your actions and decisions align with your true values.

This commitment to self-authenticity helps you build a strong and resilient ego, one that can withstand external pressures and remain true to its core essence. In this way, you can live a life that is true to yourself, free from the constraints of others' opinions and expectations.

LIKES

Our tendency to withhold "like" has contributed to a scarcity of positivity in our online interactions, hindering opportunities for connection and understanding.

The algorithms governing our digital platforms often thrive on polarization, amplifying divisions rather than encouraging empathy and unity.

Personally, I've adopted a liberal approach to liking content unless it crosses ethical boundaries.

This stance allows me to support and validate others' expressions while maintaining a respectful distance from harmful behavior.

Every post reflects someone's perspective or passion, a glimpse into their world. By embracing a culture of appreciation, we affirm their value and strengthen our bonds with one another.

Let's cultivate a spirit of generosity in our online engagements, amplifying the voices and interests of others. In doing so, we can inject positivity into a sometimes gloomy digital landscape, fostering connections and understanding.

By freely expressing our appreciation, we can nudge algorithms toward promoting harmony and connection rather than discord. Through these small gestures, we can contribute to a more peaceful and inclusive online community.

Sex

The notion that a human being can completely abstain from sex without seeking any form of sexual gratification is unrealistic.

Sexual activity is a fundamental part of human life, contributing not only to personal pleasure and intimacy but also to the continuation of the species through reproduction.

This natural drive is deeply ingrained in human biology and psychology, making it difficult for humans to completely suppress sexual urges.

Even for those who take vows of celibacy, such as monks, nuns, priests, and other religious figures across various faiths worldwide, the challenge of abstaining from sexual activity is significant.

Despite their religious commitments and disciplined lifestyles, these individuals still experience natural human desires.

The expectation that they can entirely avoid sexual thoughts or actions without any form of release is highly improbable.

Furthermore, the reality of human sexuality encompasses more than just the physical act of sex. It includes a wide range of thoughts, emotions, and behaviors that are natural and normal.

The suppression of these aspects can lead to psychological and emotional difficulties.

Therefore, the idea that anyone, regardless of their religious devotion or personal discipline, can completely abstain from all forms of sexual gratification is a misconception.

Sexual expression is an inherent part of human nature, and attempting to completely deny it is unrealistic and unhealthy.

WORDS OF WAID

It is important to recognize that the desire for sexual expression is a natural aspect of being human.

While certain individuals may choose or be required to abstain from sexual activity, the underlying human drive for sexual gratification remains.

Acknowledging this reality can lead to a more compassionate and understanding approach to human sexuality.

It is perfectly normal and acceptable to want sex, as it is a fundamental part of who we are as human beings.

LET THEM

It's important to recognize that every individual has their own unique path and set of experiences that shape their life choices.

Telling someone how to live their life can undermine their autonomy and sense of self.

People thrive when they have the freedom to make their own decisions and learn from their own experiences, even if those choices differ from what others might deem correct.

Imposing your perspective on someone else's life can lead to conflict and resentment. When individuals feel pressured to conform to another person's ideals, it creates a sense of unpeace and disharmony.

This can damage relationships and erode trust, as people will feel misunderstood or undervalued.

Furthermore, everyone's circumstances and values are different. What works well for one person might not be suitable for another.

Offering unsolicited advice can come across as judgmental and disrespectful, diminishing the recipient's confidence in their own judgment and potentially leading to further discord.

Encouraging others to find their own way fosters an environment of respect and understanding.

Supporting someone in their personal journey, rather than dictating how they should live, helps build a foundation of mutual respect and harmony.

By allowing people the space to navigate their lives, we contribute to a more peaceful and cohesive community.

Showing the true Self

Embracing your true self leads to a profound sense of freedom.

When you present yourself authentically, you shed the constraints of societal expectations and external pressures.

This act of honesty not only liberates you from the burden of pretending to be someone you're not but also fosters genuine connections with others who appreciate you for who you truly are.

Living authentically is integral to experiencing life to its fullest.

When you hide your true self, you limit your potential and diminish your experiences.

Authenticity allows you to pursue your passions and interests without fear of judgment, leading to a more fulfilling and enriched life.

It encourages a deeper engagement with the world around you, as your actions and choices reflect your genuine desires.

Indeed, freedom is essential for a fully lived life. Being true to yourself breaks the chains of conformity and self-doubt, opening the door to personal growth and self-discovery.

This freedom empowers you to explore new opportunities and embrace challenges with confidence, knowing that you are grounded in your true identity.

In essence, the journey to self-liberation through authenticity is the path to a life well- lived.

WORRYING

Worrying often consumes a significant amount of our mental and emotional energy.

When faced with a situation that we have the power to change, worrying becomes counterproductive.

Instead of allowing anxiety to dominate our thoughts, we can channel that energy into taking concrete actions to improve the circumstances.

By focusing on what we can control and making proactive changes, we can alleviate the source of our concern and create a more positive outcome.

Conversely, worrying about things beyond our control is equally unproductive.

When we encounter situations that are immutable, fretting over them only adds to our stress without offering any real solutions.

Accepting that some things are beyond our influence allows us to conserve our mental resources.

By letting go of the need to control the uncontrollable, we can redirect our focus to areas where we can make a difference and maintain a healthier state of mind.

Understanding the distinction between what we can and cannot change is crucial in managing worry effectively.

This perspective not only reduces unnecessary stress but also fosters a sense of empowerment.

WORDS OF WAID

When we recognize our ability to influence certain aspects of our lives, we feel more capable and confident.

On the other hand, accepting our limitations helps cultivate a sense of peace and resilience as we learn to navigate life's uncertainties with grace.

The key lies in mindful discernment. By assessing each situation carefully, we can determine where our efforts will be most effective.

This approach encourages us to take decisive action where possible and practice acceptance where necessary.

In doing so, we strike a balance that minimizes worry and maximizes our ability to lead a fulfilling and balanced life.

Using Logic

Using logic, one can make informed predictions about the future. By analyzing current trends, data, and patterns, logical reasoning allows individuals to foresee potential outcomes and scenarios.

For instance, economists use logical models to forecast market behavior based on historical data and current economic indicators.

Similarly, meteorologists predict weather conditions by examining atmospheric data and using established scientific principles.

Logical prediction involves a systematic approach to understanding cause and effect. When we understand how certain variables interact, we can anticipate their influence on future events.

For example, the USA and NATO countries keep sending weapons to Ukraine to fight a war they've already lost. If these so-called leaders keep acting so stupidly, one can predict an all-out war between them and Russia that will not end well because it will be a nuclear war.

Eventhough logic has its limitations and cannot account for all variables, especially those influenced by human behavior and unexpected events, despite this, logical predictions provide a valuable framework for planning and decision-making.

They enable individuals and organizations to prepare for possible future scenarios, mitigating risks and seizing opportunities.

By combining logical reasoning with flexibility and adaptability, one can navigate the uncertainties of the future more effectively.

FORGIVENESS AND APOLOGY

Most people believe that forgiveness is an act done for the benefit of others.

They think that when they forgive someone, it is a gesture that helps the person who wronged them.

However, this common perception misses the core truth about forgiveness. In reality, forgiveness is an act primarily for oneself.

When you forgive someone, you release yourself from the burden of anger, resentment, and negative emotions.

It is a personal process that allows you to find peace and move forward without the weight of past grievances holding you back.

On the other hand, an apology serves a different purpose. Apologizing to someone you have wronged provides them with the opportunity to forgive.

It opens the door for them to release their negative feelings and find closure. In this way, an apology is a powerful tool that can facilitate healing and reconciliation.

Both forgiveness and apology are intertwined in the process of emotional liberation.

While forgiveness frees you from internal turmoil, an apology can offer the same chance to someone else.

Together, they foster a healthier, more understanding relationship between individuals.

TRUE FRIEND

A true friend values honesty above all else in their relationship. They understand that their role is not just to provide comfort but to offer genuine, sincere feedback.

This commitment to truthfulness stems from a place of deep care and respect, recognizing that sugarcoating or withholding the truth can ultimately be more harmful than helpful.

Such a friend acknowledges that honesty sometimes can be uncomfortable or difficult to deliver.

They might hesitate, knowing that the truth could potentially hurt or disappoint. However, they prioritize the long-term benefits of transparency, believing that real growth and understanding come from confronting reality, even when it's tough to hear.

Furthermore, a true friend differentiates between constructive honesty and unnecessary harshness.

They aim to communicate truth with empathy and tact, ensuring that their words are aimed at supporting and guiding rather than merely criticizing.

Their intention is always to help you see a clearer picture, encourage personal growth, and foster a deeper, more authentic connection.

GOSSIPING

Respecting others' privacy is a fundamental aspect of maintaining trust and integrity in any relationship.

When we honor the personal boundaries of others, we demonstrate respect and consideration, fostering a positive and safe environment.

It is crucial to remember that everyone has a right to their own private space and personal information, and intruding upon this can lead to hurt and mistrust.

Gossiping, on the other hand, can be extremely damaging.

Engaging in gossip often reveals more about the character of the person spreading rumors than it does about the individuals being talked about.

It indicates a lack of respect and empathy and can erode the gossiper's credibility.

By choosing to gossip, one undermines their own integrity and creates an atmosphere of distrust and negativity.

The way we talk about others reflects our own values and principles.

Respecting privacy and refraining from gossiping is essential for building and maintaining strong, healthy relationships.

By valuing and upholding these principles, we contribute to a culture of respect and kindness, promoting a more harmonious and supportive community.

The value of a true friend lies in their unwavering commitment to truthfulness. They respect you enough to be honest, even when it's challenging.

This integrity forms the foundation of a strong, trusting relationship, where both parties feel secure in the knowledge that they can rely on each other for genuine, heartfelt insights.

DISCUSSING PEOPLE

Engaging in conversations that focus solely on other individuals' actions, characteristics, or personal affairs is often seen as a sign of limited intellectual curiosity.

When discussions revolve around people rather than ideas, concepts, or broader topics, it reflects a tendency to prioritize gossip and superficial details over deeper, more meaningful discourse.

This habit not only stifles personal growth but also diminishes the opportunity to explore new perspectives and expand one's understanding of the world.

On the other hand, those with a more expansive mindset are inclined to delve into discussions about ideas, philosophies, and innovative concepts.

These conversations foster intellectual stimulation and encourage critical thinking, driving personal and societal progress.

By focusing on ideas rather than individuals, people can contribute to a more enriched and enlightened discourse, promoting a culture that values thoughtful reflection and the pursuit of knowledge over trivial commentary.

EACH LIFE

Never compare lives. Each is as unique as a fingerprint.

Avoid comparing lives, as each one is uniquely distinct, much like a fingerprint.

Every individual experiences their own set of circumstances, challenges, and joys that shape their journey in ways that are incomparable to others.

Recognizing the uniqueness of each life fosters empathy and understanding.

It reminds us to appreciate the diverse paths people take and to honor the individuality of their experiences.

TEACHER AND STUDENTS

A teacher's role is not to provide direct answers but to encourage students to explore and discover solutions on their own.

By redirecting questions back to the students, teachers prompt them to think critically and engage deeply with the material.

This approach helps students develop problem-solving skills and fosters a sense of independence in their learning journey.

When individuals are encouraged to inquire within themselves, they tap into their inner resources and potential.

This introspective process allows them to reflect on their knowledge, experiences, and insights to arrive at answers.

Such self-inquiry is a powerful tool for personal growth, enabling learners to gain confidence in their abilities and trust their judgment.

This method of teaching cultivates a lifelong love for learning and curiosity.

Students learn to value the process of discovery and understand that seeking answers is a dynamic and ongoing pursuit.

By empowering learners to find answers within themselves, teachers help build resilient, self-reliant individuals who are well-equipped to face future challenges.

Moving Forward

Moving on and moving forward is an essential skill for personal growth and happiness. It is important to understand that dwelling on past events can hinder progress and keep you stuck in a cycle of regret and sorrow.

Learning to let go of what has already happened allows you to focus on the present and future, where change and improvement are possible.

The past is unchangeable, and holding on to it can be detrimental to your well-being.

Refilling on past mistakes or missed opportunities only serves to amplify feelings of sadness and frustration.

It is wise to acknowledge that the past cannot be altered and to use those experiences as lessons rather than burdens.

Focusing excessively on past events can cloud your judgment and prevent you from seeing new opportunities.

When you constantly revisit old wounds, you limit your ability to grow and appreciate the potential that lies ahead.

By choosing to let go of past grievances, you open yourself up to new experiences and personal development.

Embracing the present and looking forward to the future can bring a sense of hope and excitement.

The ability to move forward is a mark of resilience and strength.

Instead of being weighed down by what has already occurred, you can channel your energy into creating a fulfilling and positive future.

LIVING FOR OTHERS

Most people don't live for themselves.

They devote their lives to please, to impress others or to ft the norm of what society upholds, often neglecting their own needs and desires in the process.

Thisself-sacrificeleadstoaprofoundsenseofunrestanddisharmony within, as the individual's true self remains unacknowledged and unfulfilled.

Living primarily for others, in whatever capacity, creates a situation where the self is consistently ignored.

When one's own needs are perpetually sidelined in favor of others', it can result in a life that lacks balance and inner peace.

This imbalance causes emotional and psychological strain, making it difficult for individuals to find genuine contentment and satisfaction in their lives.

For example, your passion is opera but your parents want you to be a doctor to continue the family legacy.

And now, you are a well-respected surgeon, but you feel unfulfilled and unhappy.

A crucial realization that many humans have yet to achieve is the awakening of their true "I." This awakening involves becoming aware of one's own intrinsic value and understanding the importance of self-care and personal growth.

When the "I" is not awakened, people often find themselves caught in a cycle of pleasing others, which can stifle their personal development and happiness.

To attain true harmony and peace, people need to awaken to their own needs and desires.

Recognizing and nurturing one's self is essential for a balanced and fulfilling life.

When people begin to live for themselves as well as for others, they can create a more harmonious existence that honors both their individuality and their relationships with others.

The Way I See People

Try to see people not as the physical bodies they inhabit but as manifestations of the Creation Energy they are.

This perspective, rooted in the Creation Energy Teachings, offers a transformative way of seeing fellow human beings.

The teachings emphasize that every person is a unique expression of this Universal Energy, transcending the limitations of physical appearance.

The insights of Billy Meier, the Herald of this Universe, have profoundly influenced my perception.

His teachings have guided me to look beyond the superficial aspects of people and recognize their inner essence.

By internalizing these lessons, I have come to appreciate the beauty that lies within everyone, independent of their outward form.

Thanks to the wisdom imparted by these teachings, my vision of people has shifted fundamentally.

I no longer rely solely on my physical eyes to perceive others.

Instead, I connect with the energy that animates each individual, which reveals a deeper, more genuine beauty.

In embracing this view, my interactions with others have become more meaningful.

Recognizing the creation energy in everyone has fostered a sense of unity and compassion within me.

This approach to seeing beauty in all people has enriched my life, making each encounter a testament to the profound beauty of existence.

TREATED BY OTHERS

The way others treat you is largely determined by the boundaries you set for yourself.

These personal limits define how much respect and consideration you expect from others.

When you perceive yourself as inferior to someone else, you inadvertently invite them to take advantage of you.

This lack of self-worth manifests in allowing others to dominate or mistreat you. However, this dynamic changes when you recognize that no one is inherently above or beneath you.

Understanding that we all hold equal value helps foster a sense of mutual respect. This mindset shifts your interactions, ensuring that you neither belittle yourself nor place others on an undeserved pedestal.

Respecting yourself is crucial in maintaining healthy relationships and interactions.

Self-respect involves acknowledging your own worth and expecting others to do the same.

By setting firm boundaries, you communicate that you deserve to be treated with dignity and respect, thus discouraging others from overstepping these limits.

This principle extends beyond personal relationships to a broader perspective.

It implies that you should not bow down to anyone, including god if it means compromising your self-respect.

Upholding your dignity and self-worth is essential, as it reinforces that everyone is of equal value.

When a Couple Friends break up

When a couple friends break up, it's important to stay neutral and avoid taking sides.

Maintaining a neutral stance helps you avoid getting entangled in the emotional complexities of their relationship.

By not choosing sides, you preserve your friendships with both individuals without causing unnecessary tension or conflict. Refraining from giving advice during their breakup is equally crucial.

Even with the best intentions, unsolicited advice can often backfire, leading to misunderstandings or resentment.

Letting them navigate their own issues respects their autonomy and acknowledges that they are best positioned to understand their own relationship dynamics.

Never forget that couples often reconcile after a breakup.

If you've taken sides or involved yourself too deeply, you might find yourself in an awkward position once they get back together. Remaining a supportive but detached friend ensures that you can continue to be part of their lives without becoming the unwelcome third wheel.

Respecting the privacy of others' relationships fosters peace and harmony.

Recognizing that the affairs of others are none of our business helps maintain a respectful distance and promotes a more harmonious social environment.

This approach encourages healthier interactions and preserves the integrity of all friendships involved.

OUTGROW

As we grow and evolve, we naturally outgrow old habits, often without consciously realizing why.

The process of personal development involves continuous learning and adaptation, leading to a shift in our behaviors and routines.

These changes are frequently subtle, occurring gradually as we encounter new experiences and perspectives that shape our understanding of ourselves and the world around us.

Over time, our priorities and values undergo a transformation, influencing our actions and decisions.

What once seemed important or enjoyable may no longer hold the same appeal. This shift is a sign of maturation, reflecting how our goals and aspirations evolve.

As we become more attuned to our true desires and needs, we find ourselves naturally letting go of activities and behaviors that no longer serve our growth or happiness. Additionally, our social environments play a significant role in this process.

The people we interact with, the communities we engage in, and the cultural norms we are exposed to all contribute to shaping our habits.

As we move through different phases of life, we often align ourselves with new groups and surroundings that better reflect our current state of mind and aspirations.

This alignment encourages the abandonment of outdated habits in favor of those that resonate more with our present selves.

WORDS OF WAID

The shedding of old habits is a crucial part of personal evolution. It signifies progress and the continuous journey towards self-improvement.

While the reasons behind these changes might not always be immediately clear, they are an inherent aspect of growing into a more authentic and fulfilled version of ourselves.

Embracing this natural progression allows us to move forward with greater clarity and purpose.

GIVE WITHOUT EXPECTATIONS

Many Earth people have not yet fully embraced the joy of selfless giving.

True happiness and fulfillment come from acts of generosity where there is no expectation of reciprocation.

This form of giving fosters a sense of genuine contentment and connection, transcending the transactional nature often associated with exchanges.

Loving without intention means offering love freely, without seeking anything in return.

This pure form of love is not bound by conditions or expectations, allowing for deeper and more authentic relationships.

It calls for a shift from a mindset of desire and gain to one of pure, unadulterated affection.

The realization of these principles leads to profound personal and societal transformation.

When individuals begin to give and love unconditionally, they contribute to a more compassionate and harmonious world.

Such actions inspire others, creating a ripple effect that can enhance the collective human experience.

By understanding and practicing the joy of giving without expectation and the love of loving without intention, humans can unlock a higher level of existence and emotional well-being.

Do Unto Others

"Do unto others as you would have them do unto you" is a very ancient wisdom known to humanity for centuries.

This golden rule, echoed in various cultures and religions, advocates for empathy and mutual respect.

Treating others with the same kindness and consideration we desire for ourselves leads to a more compassionate and understanding society.

Despite its long-standing presence in human thought, the question remains: how many people genuinely follow this advice?

In daily life, people often struggle to practice this simple yet profound guideline.

Personal biases, misunderstandings, and conflicts overshadow the commitment to treat others with fairness and respect.

The disparity between knowing this principle and living by it highlights a significant challenge in human behavior and social interactions.

If more people embraced this wisdom wholeheartedly, true peace and harmony will flourish among us.

The potential for a more harmonious world lies in the consistent application of this rule. By fostering empathy and consideration in our interactions, we create an environment where mutual respect prevails, conflicts are minimized, and collective well-being is prioritized.

This realization and practice transform societies, leading to a more just and peaceful world.

Take Pride in What You Do For Work

Never be ashamed of what you do for a living.

It's essential to take pride in your work because it defines a significant part of who you are.

Embracing your profession with confidence fosters a sense of accomplishment and self- respect.

When you value your work, it reflects positively on your identity and contributes to your overall sense of self-worth.

If you're not proud of yourself, negative emotions like envy, regret, anger, resentment, aggression, and dissatisfaction will take root.

These feelings not only affect your well-being but also hinder your personal and professional growth.

The lack of pride leads to inner turmoil and a constant sense of shame, which can be debilitating over time.

Being ashamed of your work creates discord with those around you.

The negative emotions you harbor will be projected onto others, leading to constant misunderstandings and strained relationships.

This negativity can create a toxic environment, making it difficult for you to connect and collaborate effectively with others.

WORDS OF WAID

By taking pride in what you do, you promote peace and harmony within yourself. This positive outlook not only enhances your own life but also positively impacts the lives of those around you.

Embracing your work with pride can lead to better relationships, greater satisfaction, and a more fulfilling professional and personal life.

INTERVENTION

Intervention, as a means of influencing an individual's decisions or actions, is fundamentally flawed and inherently ineffective.

When external forces attempt to shape or control a person's choices, they often encounter resistance and resentment.

This opposition stems from a basic human desire for autonomy and self-determination. Individuals value their independence and ability to make decisions based on personal judgment and experiences.

Moreover, coerced or heavily influenced decisions lack the genuine commitment and personal conviction that come from autonomous decision-making, leading to feelings of disempowerment and dissatisfaction.

The most effective way to encourage positive change and growth in individuals is through support and empowerment rather than intervention.

By providing resources, guidance, and encouragement, we enable individuals to make informed decisions while respecting their autonomy.

This approach fosters genuine, lasting change and personal development as people learn from their experiences and develop problem-solving skills.

Honoring each person's capacity to choose their own path acknowledges their inherent dignity and potential, creating a more respectful and empowering environment for personal growth.

Silver Lining

In every situation, no matter how egregious it may be, there's always a silver lining.

Life often presents us with challenges that seem insurmountable, and in those moments, it's easy to feel overwhelmed and despondent.

However, even in the darkest times, there's a glimmer of hope waiting to be discovered. It's crucial to maintain patience during such trying times.

Patience allows us to gain perspective, take a step back and view the situation from a broader angle.

This wider perspective often reveals opportunities or positive aspects that weren't immediately apparent.

As we navigate through difficulties, the silver lining can come in various forms. It might be a lesson learned, a newfound strength, or a door opening to new possibilities.

These positive elements can profoundly impact our lives, guiding us toward growth and resilience.

The key is to trust that the silver lining will present itself in due time.

By holding on to hope and practicing patience, we can uncover the hidden blessings in every situation, transforming adversity into a stepping stone for a brighter future.

FREE WILL

Every human being possesses the inherent right to make personal choices regarding how they choose to live their lives.

This autonomy is a crucial aspect of human existence, emphasizing the significance of free will.

Each person's unique perspective and personal experiences shape their decisions, making it essential to respect their choice.

As long as a person's choices do not cause harm to others, it is imperative that they are allowed to live freely according to their values and desires.

The principle of non-interference ensures that humans can pursue their happiness and personal growth without unwarranted constraints.

Respecting this boundary is essential for maintaining personal freedoms and social harmony.

Free will stands as a fundamental right for all human beings, underscoring the importance of liberty in personal decision-making.

This right is foundational to human dignity and self-determination, allowing individuals to navigate their own paths in life.

The acknowledgment of free will reflects a commitment to respecting individual sovereignty and diversity.

In a society that values free will, interference in another's life choices is a violation of their basic human rights.

Recognizing and upholding this principle fosters a culture of mutual respect and understanding.

WORDS OF WAID

By ensuring that personal freedoms are protected, we create an environment where individuals can thrive and contribute meaningfully to the collective well-being, thus creating peace and harmony.

JESUS CHRIST

The historical figure commonly known as Jesus Christ is a fictional character.

The prophet was named Jmmanuel, who was the son of a Plejaren spiritual leader named Gabriel.

Jmmanuel also had a twin brother named Jacob/James, a fact that is purportedly omitted from the biblical texts.

Biblical references often cited in this context include Isaiah 7:14, which states, "Therefore the Lord himself will give you a sign: The virgin (unwed) will be with a child and will give birth to a son, and will call him Immanuel." This prophecy is echoed in the New Testament, specifically in Matthew 1:22-23, which notes, "All this took place to fulfill what the Lord had said through the prophet: 'The virgin (unwed) will be with a child and will give birth to a son, and they will call him Immanuel.'"

Gabriel, who is traditionally recognized as an angel in Christian doctrine, was actually a Plejaren leader.

Now, the Creation Energy or spirit of Gabriel has reincarnated and is now known as Quetzal, another Plejaren leader.

Quetzal is actively involved in guiding and assisting Billy, who is the reincarnation of the same Creation Energy that once embodied Jmmanuel.

Truly fulfilling the same mission of bringing the Creation Energy Teachings to Earth people.

THE CREATION ENERGY OF THE HUMAN BEING

The Creation Energy, or Spirit form, does not have the ability to make decisions and is free from wishes or desires.

Decisions stem from the material consciousness, and wishes and desires belong to this same realm.

The Spirit form remains neutral, merely absorbing experiences and aligning with its Creative nature.

It is inherently passive and serves as a repository of experiences rather than an active decision-maker.

Conversely, our consciousness requires continuous development and evolution.

This need for growth stands in contrast to the Spirit form's static state. It's a common misconception that we are our Spirit form, but that's not true.

Instead, we are a continuation or lineage of it, much like branches extending from a tree.

Our sense of self, or "you," refers to the ego or material consciousness, which is actively engaged in the processes of living and decision-making.

The material consciousness, also referred to as the personality, ego, or "you," exists only once in its specific form.

This aspect of our being is responsible for experiencing life, making choices, and exercising free will. It is the dynamic, evolving part of us that interacts with the world and undergoes growth throughout a single lifetime.

In contrast, the Creation Energy or Spirit form is eternal and follows the Laws of reincarnation for its evolution.

While the material consciousness ceases to exist after one lifetime, the Spirit form persists, carrying forward the accumulated wisdom and experiences from previous lives.

This cyclical process allows the Spirit to evolve continuously, adhering to the principles of reincarnation and the broader Creative order.

Our Origin and The Creation Energy Teachings

Humanity must now embrace a profound understanding of its origins, acknowledging our deep connections that extend beyond Earth.

Our lineage traces back to formidable beings from the Sirius Star system, who, filing the conflicts of their homeworld, sought refuge within our solar system on the outskirts of the Milky Way galaxy.

The Creator Overlords of Sirius played a significant role in our development, modifying our genetic makeup to include traits of destruction, aggression, and short lifespans.

These characteristics have been an inherent part of our DNA, shaping our behaviors and societal structures.

Despite our advanced civilizations, we have not yet fully evolved into genuine humans.

Our true potential remains unrealized, constrained by the genetic modifications of our ancestors. To achieve our full potential, a reversal of our genetic code is necessary.

This profound transformation is essential for us to transcend our predisposition towards aggression and destruction and to foster a more harmonious existence.

The journey towards this transformation requires a deep understanding of our true nature and the courage to change.

Fortunately, the wisdom necessary for this transformation has been bestowed upon us through the Creation Energy teachings.

These Teachings have been brought by Nokodemion, the Herald of this Universe, and transmitted through the intermediary personality of Billy Meier.

These Teachings and the main reason behind this book offer us the guidance needed to rectify our genetic imbalances and embark on a transformative path.

By embracing these Teachings, we can begin the process of healing and evolving into the true potential of humanity.

It is never too late to join this transformative journey.

Together, by embracing the wisdom and knowledge of the Creation Energy Teachings and recognizing our interconnected origins, we can change the world.

This path offers hope and the possibility of a brighter future, where humanity transcends its inherent predispositions and realizes its true potential.

Let us unite in this endeavor to create a better world for ourselves and future generations.

No Divine Power

Human beings are inherently autonomous and possess the unique ability to control their own destinies.

Each individual holds the power to make decisions and shape their life's path according to their own values and aspirations.

This fundamental aspect of human nature underscores the profound responsibility we have over our own existence.

As the sole architects of our lives, we are not subject to any external forces that can dictate our choices. Truly, there's no God.

While external circumstances can influence and challenge us, the ultimate power to navigate these influences lies within us.

Our thoughts, actions, and responses to life's challenges are all within our control, reinforcing the idea that we are the masters of our own lives.

Embracing this truth empowers us to take charge of our lives with confidence and purpose.

It encourages a proactive mindset where personal growth and self-improvement become central themes.

Recognizing that no one else can control our destiny inspires us to pursue our goals with determination and resilience, knowing that we hold the key to our own success and that nothing happens by the grace of a god because such does not exit.

The realization that we alone govern our lives instills a sense of freedom and empowerment.

It reminds us that we are capable of overcoming obstacles and achieving greatness through our own efforts.

By accepting this truth, we lead more fulfilling and purposeful lives driven by our own passions and convictions.

Refrain From Attacking One Another

It is important not to attack fellow human beings who are trying to raise awareness and awaken others to various issues.

These individuals are working towards a common goal and should be seen as allies rather than adversaries.

By acknowledging their efforts, we recognize that we are all on the same team, striving for a better understanding and positive change in society.

Encouragement is crucial for those who take on the challenging task of helping others to awaken.

This journey is fraught with difficulties, and support from like-minded individuals makes a significant difference. Instead of criticism, offering encouragement helps to sustain their motivation and reinforces the collective mission: We are all in this together.

Recognizing the shared goal and providing support creates a more unified and effective effort. Working together and lifting each other up fosters a collaborative environment where progress can be made more efficiently.

In this way, we can better navigate the challenges and achieve the desired outcomes as a cohesive group.

In Love With Your Own Voice

It's easy to become enamored with the sound of your own voice, particularly when you are confident in what you have to say.

However, it's crucial to remember that effective communication involves not just speaking but also listening.

When you dominate conversations, you might miss out on valuable insights and perspectives that others have to offer.

Letting others speak fosters a more inclusive and balanced dialogue. It shows that you value and respect the contributions of those around you.

By actively listening and giving others the space to express their thoughts, you create a more collaborative and enriching environment for everyone involved.

In addition, encouraging others to share their ideas can lead to more innovative solutions and a deeper understanding of the topics at hand. By not monopolizing the conversation, you allow for a diversity of opinions and experiences to surface, which can enhance the quality and depth of the discussion.

The goal is to create a conversation where all voices are heard and respected, leading to more meaningful and productive interactions. This creates a more harmonious environment for those involved.

STARSTRUCK

Starstruck behavior is a form of mental imbalance. It involves an excessive admiration or obsession with celebrities or public figures to the point where it can distort one's perception of reality.

This fixation leads individuals to neglect their own lives, aspirations, and self-worth, prioritizing the lives of those they idolize instead.

Placing another human being on a pedestal is inherently problematic. It creates unrealistic expectations for both the admirer and the idolized individual.

The admirer may develop an unhealthy dependency on the actions or opinions of the idol, while the idolized person is unfairly burdened with living up to an idealized and often unattainable standard.

This dynamic can be detrimental to both parties, fostering disappointment, disillusionment, and emotional distress.

Recognizing and addressing starstruck behavior is crucial for maintaining mental well- being. It's important to admire others' achievements without losing sight of one's own identity and values.

Encouraging a balanced perspective helps individuals appreciate their own worth and contributions, preventing the unhealthy elevation of others to an exalted status that can lead to mental and emotional turmoil.

LIFE

Nothing in life holds more value than life itself. Life serves as a classroom where the Creation Energy of human beings can evolve and grow.

Unlike the common misconception that life should be easy, the true purpose of life lies in encountering challenges, making mistakes, and learning from these experiences.

These life experiences are essential for personal and collective growth.

Mistakes provide opportunities for learning and development, shaping individuals into more understanding and compassionate beings.

It is through these trials that humans gain wisdom and resilience, underscoring the importance of preserving every life.

Therefore, the death penalty should be eradicated from our planet.

Life is a precious gift imbued with love, and no one deserves to have it taken away, regardless of their actions.

Every individual, regardless of their deeds, should have the chance to learn, grow, and redeem themselves, reflecting the intrinsic value and sanctity of life.

MOTHERS

Mothers are a child's first teachers.

From the earliest moments of life, they play a crucial role in shaping their children's understanding of the world, imparting fundamental lessons and nurturing their development.

Through their guidance and care, mothers provide the essential foundation for learning and growth.

They teach not only practical skills but also instill values, morals, and a sense of curiosity, laying the groundwork for a lifetime of education and personal development.

Politics

Politics functions as a divisive institution, creating rifts among people rather than fostering unity.

It thrives on differences in opinion, ideology, and interests, often leading to conflicts and misunderstandings among the populace.

This division can hinder collective progress and cooperation, making it crucial for people to be aware of these dynamics.

For the people of Earth to truly unite, it is essential to recognize and address the divisive nature of politics.

By paying closer attention to how political structures and agendas can manipulate and polarize societies, individuals can better understand the underlying forces at play.

This awareness can empower people to find common ground and work together towards shared goals rather than being driven apart by political differences.

Unity among people requires a concerted effort to look beyond the divisive tactics of politics.

By fostering open dialogue, mutual respect, and a focus on common interests, individuals can resist divisive influences and work towards a more harmonious and collaborative world.

Understanding and addressing the role of politics in creating division is a critical step in achieving true unity and collective progress.

MILITARY DRAFT

A military draft should be rejected by every human being. Compulsory conscription undermines the fundamental principle of free will, which is a birthright for all human beings.

The freedom to choose whether or not to participate in military service is essential for maintaining personal autonomy and integrity.

Forcing individuals into military service against their will strips them of their inherent right to make decisions about their own lives.

This imposition not only violates personal freedoms but also can lead to significant moral and psychological conflicts.

Every person should have the opportunity to decide for themselves whether they are willing to take part in armed conflict based on their own values and morals.

Respecting free will is crucial for the dignity and respect of all human beings. By rejecting a military draft, society upholds the principle that each person has the right to control their own destiny.

Ensuring that participation in the military is a voluntary choice supports the fundamental human rights of autonomy and self-determination, which are essential for a just and free society.

COMPETITION

Competition leads to division and disrupts peace and harmony. It fosters an environment where individuals are pitted against each other, which can breed resentment and conflict.

When competition is emphasized, it undermines the sense of community and cooperation that is essential for a harmonious society.

It is important to avoid instilling a competitive mindset in our children. Teaching them to compete rather than collaborate can have detrimental effects on their mental and emotional well-being.

Instead of fostering a spirit of teamwork and mutual support, it encourages a focus on outdoing others, which can lead to stress, anxiety, and unhealthy comparisons.

Promoting cooperation and collective growth is far more beneficial for our children's development.

By emphasizing collaboration and empathy over competition, we can help them build strong, supportive relationships and create a more peaceful and harmonious society.

Encouraging children to work together rather than against each other nurtures their innate potential for kindness and understanding, which are crucial for a healthy and balanced life.

IGNORING AND MOVING ON

Learning to ignore and move on is an essential skill for maintaining mental peace.

Dwelling on negative thoughts or past grievances only serves to clutter your mind and hinder personal growth.

It's important to recognize when to let go and focus on more positive and productive aspects of life.

Allowing someone to occupy space in your mind without contributing anything positive can be detrimental to your well-being. No one should have the power to live rent-free in your thoughts, especially if their presence causes stress or unhappiness.

By consciously choosing to dismiss these unproductive thoughts, you can reclaim your mental space and emotional energy.

Prioritizing your mental health means actively deciding what and who deserves your attention.

Moving on from negative influences allows you to invest your time and energy in more fulfilling and uplifting pursuits.

This practice not only enhances your overall well-being but also empowers you to create a healthier and more positive mindset.

LISTEN WITHOUT GIVING YOUR OPINION

Developing the ability to listen without immediately interjecting with one's own opinion is a valuable skill.

Often, individuals simply seek someone who will lend them an empathetic ear without offering judgment or unsolicited advice. By actively listening, we demonstrate respect for the speaker and create a safe space for them to express themselves freely.

Sometimes, the most meaningful support we can provide is through silent understanding.

People may not always be seeking solutions or advice. They may simply need to vent or share their thoughts and feelings.

By refraining from inserting our own opinions, we allow the speaker to feel heard and validated, which can be incredibly empowering and comforting.

It's important to recognize when our input is genuinely solicited. While offering our perspective can be beneficial in certain situations, it's essential to wait until we're invited to share it.

By respecting boundaries and being mindful of the speaker's intentions, we can ensure that our contributions are welcomed and constructive. This approach fosters deeper connections and promotes mutual respect in our interactions with others.

Bond Between People

The connections forged between human beings endure beyond a single lifetime. These bonds, whether with family, friends, or partners, hold the potential to transcend the boundaries of time and space.

It is incumbent upon us to nurture and strengthen these relationships rather than resorting to superficial or insincere interactions.

Genuine bonds are built on a foundation of trust, honesty, and mutual respect.

Fostering authenticity in our relationships requires sincere effort and a willingness to be vulnerable.

By investing time and energy into cultivating meaningful connections, we can create enduring ties that enrich our lives and those of others.

While it may be tempting to fabricate or embellish relationships for personal gain, true fulfillment comes from genuine connections.

Authenticity fosters deeper understanding and empathy, laying the groundwork for lasting bonds that withstand the test of time.

By prioritizing sincerity over superficiality, we can build relationships that enrich our lives and leave a lasting legacy of love and connection.

FOLLOWER

It's imperative not to blindly follow any individual solely based on their status or influence. Every person holds equal inherent worth, and no one should be idolized or unquestioningly obeyed.

Instead of focusing on individuals, it's essential to critically evaluate their teachings and actions to determine their compatibility with our own values and beliefs.

True guidance lies not in blindly following individuals but in discerning the wisdom within their teachings. When considering someone's teachings, it's crucial to assess whether their principles align with our own moral compass.

Only by critically evaluating their teachings can we integrate those that resonate with our values into our lives, fostering personal growth and development.

Following someone's teachings that align with our values empowers us to make informed decisions and lead lives that are true to ourselves.

By maintaining autonomy and discernment, we can navigate the complexities of life with integrity and authenticity.

Rather than blindly adhering to authority figures, we can draw inspiration from their teachings while remaining steadfast in our commitment to our own principles and beliefs.

Self-Respect

Believing that everything in life occurs solely by the grace of a god undermines one's sense of self-worth and agency as a human being. It reinforces a passive acceptance of fate and diminishes the importance of individual effort and achievement.

When we attribute all our successes and failures solely to divine intervention, we diminish our own role in shaping our lives and fulfilling our potential.

Self-respect is rooted in recognizing and valuing one's own abilities, efforts, and accomplishments. By attributing all achievements solely to external forces, individuals inadvertently diminish their own sense of agency and self-worth.

Genuine self-respect requires acknowledging and celebrating our own contributions to our successes rather than attributing them solely to divine intervention.

Genuine respect for others stems from a foundation of self-respect. If one lacks respect for oneself as a capable and competent individual, it becomes challenging to extend genuine respect to others.

Self-respect provides the basis for treating others with empathy, compassion, and dignity, recognizing their inherent worth as fellow human beings.

Therefore, fostering a healthy sense of self-respect is essential for cultivating meaningful and authentic relationships with others.

ADDICTION

Witnessing a loved one struggle with addiction can be profoundly distressing, but ultimately, the decision to seek help and overcome addiction rests solely with the individual.

Despite our best intentions, attempts to intervene or control their behavior are often futile.

Only when the individual themselves acknowledges their need for change and commit to recovery can meaningful progress be made.

Respecting the autonomy of the individual is paramount, even in the face of destructive behavior.

Each person has the right to make decisions about their own life, including whether to seek help for addiction.

While it may be agonizing to stand by and watch them harm themselves, forcibly intervening can exacerbate their resistance and strain the relationship further.

Accepting the limitations of our influence brings a measure of peace amidst the turmoil of watching a loved one struggle.

While we may offer support, guidance, and encouragement, the ultimate choice to seek help and pursue recovery lies with them.

Redirecting our focus towards self-care and setting healthy boundaries can help mitigate the emotional toll of witnessing a loved one's addiction.

Supernatural

The concept of the supernatural arises from phenomena that seem inexplicable or beyond the realms of scientific understanding.

However, upon closer examination and thorough investigation, these occurrences can be explained by natural laws and processes.

What initially appears mysterious or otherworldly often becomes comprehensible through scientific inquiry and empirical evidence.

Human understanding continually evolves as we uncover the underlying principles governing the universe.

What was once deemed supernatural will later be revealed as a natural phenomenon as our knowledge and comprehension of the world expand.

Through observation, experimentation, and analysis, we strive to demystify the unknown and shed light on previously enigmatic phenomena. Through the Energy Teachings of Billy, many universal laws are explained.

For instance, this Universe called the Dern Universe is composed of 6 other Universes and has another twin universe called the Dal Universe...

Embracing the truth that everything is natural once it's understood encourages the pursuit of knowledge and a deeper appreciation for the intricacies of the natural world.

Rather than attributing events to mystical or divine forces, we can approach them with curiosity and a scientific mindset, seeking to uncover the underlying mechanisms at play.

This perspective fosters a sense of wonder and awe at the inherent order and complexity of the universe. And the Creation Energy Teachings are a great source of information in regard to this Universe and everything in it.

Focus On Your Life

Directing your focus inward toward your own life is essential for personal growth and development. While it may be tempting to become preoccupied with the lives of others, true evolution occurs when we prioritize our own journey.

Comparing ourselves to others or focusing on their lives detracts from our own progress and hinders our ability to reach our full potential.

Each individual's evolution is unique and depends solely on their own actions, choices, and experiences. While external influences may play a role in shaping our path, ultimately, the responsibility for our growth lies within ourselves.

By cultivating self-awareness, setting meaningful goals, and taking intentional steps toward self-improvement, we can chart a course toward personal evolution and fulfillment.

Redirecting our focus towards our own lives empowers us to take ownership of our journey and embrace our individuality.

Rather than being consumed by the lives of others, we can channel our energy toward self-discovery, self-improvement, and self-fulfillment.

Embracing this mindset fosters a sense of empowerment and autonomy, allowing us to thrive on our own terms and create a life that reflects our true desires and aspirations.

LISTEN WITHOUT INTERRUPTING

Civility hinges on the art of listening attentively, giving others the space to express themselves fully without interruption. By lending our ears to others, we convey respect and consideration, fostering an environment of mutual understanding and empathy.

The act of listening goes beyond mere silence. It entails genuine engagement and receptiveness to the thoughts and feelings of others.

Allowing individuals to finish their thoughts without interruption is a sign of respect for their perspective and autonomy.

It acknowledges their right to be heard and valued, regardless of differences in opinion or background. In a civil exchange, each voice is given the opportunity to contribute to the conversation, enriching the dialogue with diverse viewpoints and insights.

Practicing attentive listening not only promotes civility but also cultivates deeper connections and rapport with others.

By demonstrating a willingness to listen and understand, we strengthen relationships and build trust, laying the groundwork for constructive communication and collaboration.

In a world often characterized by divisiveness and discord, the simple act of listening can serve as a powerful catalyst for fostering harmony and mutual respect.

I Don't do Protest

Choosing not to engage in protests stems from the fact that they are often met with suppression by those in positions of power.

What this world needs is a revolution rooted in the truth, the Silent revolution of Truth.

This new perspective will shift the focus from outward demonstrations of dissent to an internal awakening and transformation of individual and collective awareness.

By elevating consciousness to a higher level of understanding and empathy, individuals can challenge existing power structures and foster a more just and equitable society.

While protests may serve as a catalyst for social change, the true revolution lies in the awakening of human consciousness to universal truths and principles.

This inner revolution transcends traditional modes of activism and offers a pathway toward lasting transformation and progress.

By embracing the power of truth and consciousness, individuals can collectively pave the way for a brighter and more harmonious future for all.

ORGASM II

The point where Everything meets Nothing.

ROOT FOR THE POOR AND REJOICE IN THE WINNING OF THE POWERFUL

There's a paradoxical aspect to human nature: while we may empathize with the struggles of the underprivileged, we often find ourselves celebrating the victories of the powerful.

This incongruity speaks to the complexity of our societal values and the dynamics of power and privilege.

Despite our professed support for the disadvantaged, our actions sometimes reveal a bias towards those in positions of authority and influence.

Our inclination to root for the underdog stems from a sense of justice and fairness, as we recognize the inherent challenges faced by those who lack resources or opportunities.

We empathize with their struggles and champion their resilience in the face of adversity.

However, when it comes to celebrating the successes of the powerful, our admiration is influenced by factors such as wealth, status, and achievement rather than the principles of equity and justice.

Navigating this dichotomy requires introspection and a commitment to aligning our values with our actions.

While it's natural to admire success, we must also question the systems and structures that perpetuate inequality and privilege.

By consciously supporting initiatives that uplift the marginalized and challenge the status quo, we can strive to bridge the gap between our ideals and our behavior, ultimately fostering a more equitable and compassionate society.

Victory Over The Self

The most significant triumph one can achieve is not external conquest but rather the mastery of oneself.

This internal victory holds profound significance because, in many ways, we are our own greatest adversaries.

The obstacles we face within ourselves—such as self-doubt, fear, and insecurity—often prove to be more formidable than any external challenge.

Conquering the self involves confronting and overcoming our inner demons, transforming weaknesses into strengths, and aligning our actions with our values and aspirations.

It requires self-awareness, discipline, and resilience to navigate the complexities of our own minds and emotions.

This journey of self-mastery is lifelong and requires continual introspection and growth. While external achievements may bring temporary satisfaction, true fulfillment comes from inner peace and harmony.

By triumphing over our own limitations and inner conflicts, we unlock our full potential and experience a profound sense of liberation and empowerment.

The victory over the self is not only the most challenging but also the most rewarding, as it lays the foundation for a life of purpose, authenticity, and fulfillment.

THE GOD BELIEVER

Beliefs hold immense power over human behavior, capable of inspiring both acts of compassion and devastating violence.

The danger lies in the unquestioning obedience to beliefs, even when they dictate actions that contradict fundamental moral values.

This blind adherence to beliefs leads individuals to commit unspeakable acts, rationalizing their actions as divine mandates.

The influence of beliefs extends beyond individual autonomy, shaping societal norms and behaviors on a larger scale.

When individuals perceive their beliefs as absolute truths, they feel compelled to impose them on others, often with dire consequences.

This lack of critical examination and open-mindedness perpetuates a cycle of violence and oppression fueled by the conviction that one's beliefs are superior and beyond reproach.

The human capacity for reason and empathy is overshadowed by the overwhelming influence of belief systems.

This highlights the urgent need for critical thinking, skepticism, and dialogue to challenge entrenched beliefs and promote understanding and tolerance.

By acknowledging the limitations of our beliefs and embracing knowledge, humility and empathy, we can work toward a world where differences are respected and violence in the name of belief becomes a relic of the past.

FEAR NO ONE BUT YOURSELF

Fear should not be directed towards others but rather towards the obstacles and limitations within oneself.

This principle underscores the importance of self-awareness and introspection in navigating life's challenges.

While external threats may elicit fear, the greatest source of apprehension often lies within our own minds and insecurities.

Directing fear toward oneself serves as a reminder of the power and agency we possess in shaping our lives.

It encourages introspection and self-examination, prompting us to confront our fears, doubts, and shortcomings head-on.

By acknowledging and addressing our innermost fears, we can cultivate resilience and fortitude, empowering ourselves to overcome obstacles and pursue our goals with confidence and determination.

Embracing this mindset liberates us from the shackles of external intimidation and empowers us to take control of our destiny.

Rather than being governed by the fear of others' judgments or actions, we become the masters of our own fate. By prioritizing self-awareness and self-mastery, we can navigate life with courage and conviction, unencumbered by the fear of external influences.

Anger

Allowing anger to fester within oneself will have detrimental effects on both mental well-being and physical health.

It's essential to recognize that harboring anger not only affects our psyche but also compromises our overall health and vitality.

Thus, it's imperative to strive towards eliminating anger from our lives and cultivating a sense of inner peace and harmony.

Learning to let go of resentment and hate is a transformative process that requires introspection and self-awareness.

By releasing the grip of anger, we free ourselves from the burdens of negativity and toxicity.

Instead of clinging to grudges and grievances, we can choose forgiveness and compassion, paving the way for healing and reconciliation.

The more we hold onto anger, the more it consumes us, clouding our judgment and distorting our perception of reality.

By releasing anger and embracing forgiveness, we reclaim control over our emotions and restore balance to our lives.

Cultivating a mindset of peace and acceptance allows us to navigate life's challenges with grace and resilience, fostering a sense of inner tranquility and well-being.

LYING

Lying represents a cowardly evasion of responsibility, as it entails avoiding the consequences of our actions by deceiving others.

By resorting to falsehoods, we betray a lack of courage and integrity, opting for short- term comfort over long-term honesty.

Moreover, lying deprives others of their autonomy, as it withholds essential information necessary for informed decision-making.

When we lie, we undermine the free will of our fellow human beings by denying them access to the truth.

By withholding crucial facts, we manipulate the choices of others, denying them the opportunity to make decisions based on accurate information.

Thisdeceitfulbehaviorerodestrustandunderminesthefoundations of healthy relationships, leading to discord and resentment.

Conversely, speaking the truth empowers both ourselves and others, fostering transparency and integrity in our interactions.

By honoring the truth, we uphold the dignity and autonomy of our fellow human beings, allowing them to make informed decisions in alignment with their values and aspirations.

Embracing honesty not only cultivates trust and authenticity but also strengthens the fabric of our connections, fostering a culture of openness and accountability.

Sex Partner

Who you're attracted to and who you choose to date are deeply personal matters that belong solely to you. You are under no obligation to justify or explain your romantic preferences to anyone, including close relatives. Similarly, the decision of who to engage in sexual activity with is a private aspect of your life that is entirely your own business. Your life belongs to you and you alone, and you have the power to live it on your own terms.

Taking ownership of your life means reclaiming the power to make decisions that align with your desires and values. It entails asserting your autonomy and refusing to be swayed by the opinions or expectations of others. Embracing this mindset allows you to live authentically and unapologetically, free from the constraints of societal norms or external judgment.

In the grand scheme of your life, the opinions and judgments of others are merely background noise. What truly matters is your own happiness, fulfillment, and sense of self-empowerment. By prioritizing your own well-being and following your heart's desires, you can lead a life that is true to yourself, regardless of the opinions or expectations of others.

Piyali

Expressing love and appreciation for others shouldn't be postponed until they have passed on.

It's important to show love and gratitude while our loved ones are still among us. With this sentiment in mind, I'd like to take a moment to acknowledge the remarkable qualities of a truly special woman, my sister Piyali.

She possesses a voice that is nothing short of extraordinary. I call her the "one with the Angelic voice."

Her voice has a transcendent quality that captivates all who hear it, transporting listeners to a realm of pure bliss.

I want to honor her in this book with the recognition and admiration she deserves.

Dear sister, you embody the qualities of a future mother of the millennium, exuding warmth, kindness, and boundless love in all that you do.

In celebrating her, I acknowledge the profound impact she has on those around her and the legacy of love and inspiration she leaves in her wake.

Let us cherish the opportunity to express our love and appreciation for the remarkable people in our lives, ensuring that they know just how deeply they are valued and cherished.

The Silent Revolution of Truth

In the awakening of the First wave, formerly reserved and timid human beings find themselves emboldened by their newfound purpose.

Their once-contained knowledge now bursts forth with confidence, no longer confined within themselves.

Across the landscape, the Teachings of Billy regarding the Creation Energy resonate ever more strongly, permeating minds and hearts alike.

As this truth gains traction, its presence becomes palpable, actively advancing its cause and spreading its influence.

With each passing moment, the dawn of the New Age draws nearer, beckoning those attuned to its call.

The transformation of once-shy souls into beacons of knowledge and confidence heralds a shift in consciousness, marking the beginning of a profound journey.

As the light of awareness spreads, the boundaries of understanding expand, illuminating pathways to greater truths and deeper insights.

In this burgeoning era, the veil of ignorance is gradually lifted, revealing the inherent interconnectedness of all things.

WORDS OF WAID

As more people start to embrace their roles as stewards of Creation Energy, they find themselves woven into the fabric of a universal tapestry, each thread contributing to the vibrant mosaic of existence.

With each step forward, the momentum of awakening grows, propelling humanity ever closer to the realization of its collective purpose.

Welcome, then, to this transformative moment in history, where the whispers of Truth swell into a resounding chorus.

It is a time of empowerment, discovery, and unity—a time to embrace the boundless potential of the human spirit as it embarks on a journey toward enlightenment and fulfillment.

Taking an Elevator

When you find yourself in an elevator with other people, don't hesitate to say hello and engage in a friendly conversation.

A simple greeting can go a long way in making a positive impression. Asking someone about their day shows that you care and are interested in their well-being.

Taking the time to interact with others in such a confined space helps create a sense of connection and community.

It may seem like a small gesture, but showing kindness and interest in others' lives fosters mutual respect and understanding.

These brief interactions can break the monotony of daily routines and brighten someone's day.

By consistently greeting and conversing with people in shared spaces, you contribute to a more harmonious environment.

This practice of friendliness and goodwill builds lasting relationships and creates a more positive atmosphere wherever you go.

Such simple acts of kindness can have a lasting impact, promoting peace and harmony in your daily interactions.

After a Breakup

After a breakup, my feelings for the person transformed from romantic love into a deep sense of sisterhood.

I begin to view them as a sister, someone I care for in a different but equally profound way.

My love for them evolves, becoming more about their well-being and happiness than about a romantic connection.

Despite the end of our romantic relationship, the memories we created and the love we once shared remain precious to me.

I cherish the time we spent together, and those moments continue to hold a special place in my being.

My affection for them doesn't diminish. It simply takes on a new form that is filled with respect and admiration.

In this new phase, I see myself as their biggest supporter. My love for them is unwavering, and I genuinely want to see them happy and thriving.

I will always be there for them, rooting for their success and joy, just as I would for a sibling.

I hold no hard feelings or resentments towards them whatsoever. What's past is past.

WHEN MEETING A FELLOW HUMAN BEING

Whenever I meet someone, I make it a point to find something I genuinely find nice to compliment them on.

It could be their radiant smile, the striking color of their eyes, or the stylish outfit they're wearing.

There's always something beautiful about each person if you take the time to look.

Acknowledging these small details and expressing appreciation for them fosters a sense of peace, happiness, and harmony.

It creates a positive connection between you and the other person, making them feel seen and valued. This simple act of kindness can have a profound impact on their day.

The love and attention you show by offering a sincere compliment can leave a lasting impression.

It often leads to a meaningful and memorable connection, potentially paving the way for a lifelong friendship.

In this way, your gesture of appreciation not only uplifts the other person but also enriches your own social interactions.

My Approach To Life

I approach everything with a neutral mindset, recognizing the diversity of perspectives around me.

It's unrealistic to expect unanimous agreement on all matters, and, in fact, life would be monotonous without differing viewpoints.

This variety in thought and opinion enriches our experiences and fosters personal growth.

Therefore, I encourage everyone to speak their truth freely. It's important to share your perspective openly without the fear of dissent.

At the same time, it is crucial not to take disagreements personally.

Divergent views are not a reflection of personal animosity but an opportunity for dialogue and understanding.

We are all here to teach and learn from one another.

By sharing our insights and experiences, we contribute to a collective wisdom that benefits everyone.

This exchange of ideas is foundational to our personal and communal development.

Showing others your perspective while allowing them to share theirs creates a more harmonious and peaceful humanity.

It fosters respect, empathy, and collaboration, leading to a more inclusive and understanding world.

By embracing this approach, we can all contribute to a richer, more diverse community.

Soon or Later

At some point in the future, humanity will need to move beyond its current preoccupation with material wealth and possessions.

This shift is crucial for the long-term well-being of both individuals and society as a whole.

The endless pursuit of material goods leads to a cycle of dissatisfaction and environmental degradation, making it clear that this path is unsustainable.

In contrast, embracing spirituality offers a more fulfilling and sustainable way of living.

Spirituality encourages people to seek deeper meaning and connection beyond the superficial allure of materialism.

By focusing on inner growth, compassion, and a sense of interconnectedness, human beings can find greater peace and contentment.

This shift in perspective can also lead to more harmonious and supportive communities.

This transformation from materialism to spirituality is not just beneficial but necessary.

As the pressures on our planet increase, fostering a more spiritual approach to life will help mitigate many of the challenges we face.

It can inspire actions that prioritize the health of our environment and the well-being of all life forms.

By embracing spirituality, humanity can create a more balanced, peaceful, harmonious and sustainable future.

Death

I have faced death so many times that its presence no longer disturbs me. This repeated exposure has brought me to a profound understanding: when we truly grasp the nature of death, our appreciation for life intensifies.

Recognizing the fleeting nature of our existence prompts us to cherish each moment more deeply, savoring the experiences and connections that make life meaningful.

Death should not be perceived as the ultimate end but rather as a transition. Life itself is eternal, and death is merely the conclusion of one chapter, much like birth signifies the beginning of another.

This cyclical view of existence helps us see death not as a termination but as a natural part of life's ongoing journey.

By viewing death as the opposite of birth rather than the end of life, we transform our perspective.

This understanding encourages us to live more fully, embracing the continuity and boundlessness of existence.

Knowing that life does not end with death allows us to diminish feelings of jealousy and envy as we realize that if our goals are not achieved in one lifetime, there are many more opportunities ahead.

Just as we cannot eat everything at a buffet in one day, we cannot accomplish everything in a single lifetime.

Accepting this helps us to pace ourselves and find peace in life.

Each lifetime is a chance to experience, learn, and grow, contributing to our eternal existence and the evolution of the Creation Energy.

This realization enables us to live with greater freedom and purpose, appreciating each day as a unique and valuable part of an endless journey.

Repetition

To effectively show people the truth, it is necessary to repeat the truth multiple times. The first time they encounter it, they are likely to ignore it entirely.

This initial exposure often fails to make an impression, as it may seem irrelevant or insignificant.

The second time they see the truth, they may not remember having encountered it before.

This lack of recollection means the message still hasn't taken root in their minds. Familiarity hasn't yet developed, and the information doesn't stand out.

It is around the fourth time that they begin to consider that they have encountered this information previously, which prompts them to ponder its significance. With the fifth repetition, they start to delve deeper into the idea, thinking critically about it.

By the sixth time, they are motivated to investigate further and verify its validity themselves. Finally, by the seventh encounter, they have internalized the truth to such an extent that they feel confident enough to share it with others.

OVERPOPULATION

We are facing an overpopulation problem that has significant consequences for our planet. As the global population grows, the demand for various resources increases correspondingly.

People require food, water, housing, and numerous other goods and services, all of which necessitate substantial amounts of natural resources to produce and maintain.

The extraction and utilization of these resources involve extensive processing. This processing, in turn, demands considerable energy inputs.

To meet this energy requirement, we primarily rely on fossil fuels, which, when burned, release greenhouse gases into the atmosphere.

These gases include carbon dioxide, methane, and nitrous oxide, all of which contribute to the greenhouse effect.

The greenhouse effect is a natural process where greenhouse gases trap heat within the Earth's atmosphere.

While they allow sunlight to enter the atmosphere freely, they hinder the escape of heat back into space. This trapping of heat leads to an overall increase in the Earth's temperature, thus global warming.

Global warming, or climate change, is intrinsically linked to our energy consumption patterns driven by population growth.

As more people require more goods, the subsequent increase in energy production results in higher greenhouse gas emissions.

Addressing overpopulation and its associated resource demands is crucial in mitigating the adverse effects of climate change and ensuring a sustainable future for our planet. The belief in "go forth and multiply" is misguided.

Gaining a better understanding of life through the Creation Energy Teachings can help addressing the overpopulation crisis we're currently facing.

A Job You Don't Like

Working in a job you don't enjoy can lead to significant distress and negatively impact your overall well-being.

This dissatisfaction often manifests in increased irritability and a pervasive sense of unhappiness.

Over time, the stress and discomfort of working in an unfulfilling role can take a toll on both your mental and physical health.

It's crucial to recognize these signs and consider seeking alternative employment that aligns better with your interests and passions.

The importance of job satisfaction can't be overstated.

When you find yourself dreading work every day, it's a clear indication that a change is necessary.

Prioritizing your well-being should always come first, as your happiness and mental health are invaluable.

Exploring new job opportunities, even if it feels daunting, is a vital step towards a more fulfilling and balanced life.

However, the reality is that sometimes, the job you dislike might be your only source of income.

In such cases, it's essential to remember that there are always options available, even if they aren't immediately apparent.

It might require creative thinking and careful planning, but finding a way to transition to a more satisfying career is possible.

Life is full of challenges, and overcoming them leads to personal growth and a deeper understanding of your capabilities.

WORDS OF WAID

Life's journey is about facing and conquering obstacles. Having trust in your ability to handle whatever comes your way is key.

And always remember that no God is going to help you because such truly doesn't exist. However, this resilience and determination are part of the beauty of life.

Nothing can happen to you that you can't handle is the truth.

By staying positive and proactive, you can navigate through tough times and move toward a future that brings you joy and fulfillment.

Always try to do something you enjoy doing.

THE TEACHINGS

The Creation Energy Teachings represent a profound opportunity for peace among humanity.

These teachings have a significant impact on our thinking patterns, encouraging positivity and reducing tendencies toward aggression.

They guide us toward a mindset that values harmony and understanding, fostering a collective sense of tranquility.

One of the core principles of these teachings is to cultivate happiness for others' successes, a Teamproud mentality.

By doing so, they help eliminate feelings of envy, hatred and the desire for retaliation or revenge, promoting a more neutral and fair judgment of situations based on understanding and logic.

This shift in perspective is crucial for building a society rooted in compassion and mutual respect, where people support each other's growth and achievements.

Hope you all join us soon.

Others' Aggression

The aggression of others is not yours to bear.

These negative emotions and actions belong to them, not to you.

Observing them without taking them on as your own allows you to maintain your own inner calm.

When you encounter aggression, let it pass by without getting entangled in it.

Approach these situations with love and understanding, recognizing that this aggression does not define you or require your involvement.

By doing so, you safeguard your peace and avoid unnecessary conflict. This approach fosters peace and harmony among people.

By not reacting to aggression with more negativity, you contribute to a more balanced and tranquil environment.

Your calm and loving response can help to diffuse tension and promote more positive interactions.

It takes practice, but it's totally achievable.

Take nothing personally - Not even personal attacks.

In Everything

In every situation, strive to choose peace and harmony.

This way of being fosters a more serene environment and encourages positive interactions with others.

By prioritizing peace, you create a space where mutual respect and understanding can thrive, leading to more constructive and fulfilling relationships.

Allow others to express themselves freely, regardless of whether you agree with their viewpoints.

Everyone has the same right to voice their thoughts and feelings.

By listening with an open mind, you demonstrate respect for their perspective and reinforce the value of diverse opinions.

This approach not only strengthens your connections but also broadens your own understanding.

When people are talking, it's essential to listen attentively.

Their words matter, and your patience and willingness to wait for your turn to speak show that you value what they have to say.

This practice not only enhances communication but also fosters a sense of respect and empathy, which are crucial for meaningful interactions.

In conversations, don't aim to win arguments but rather to learn something new. Every interaction offers a lesson, and it's up to you to recognize and embrace it.

WORDS OF WAID

Treat people as you wish to be treated, and remember that the way you allow others to treat you sets a precedent.

By offering your true sentiments openly, you will feel more liberated and genuine.

Recognizing the inherent love and creativity in everyone and everything around you can greatly enrich your experiences and relationships.

LIKE A CAMERA

Everyone is like a camera that records and sees what is within its field of view. Each person captures their own unique perspective on the world around them.

However, one's vision can be greatly expanded by sharing and receiving perspectives from others.

This exchange enriches our understanding and broadens our horizons, allowing us to see beyond our own limited viewpoints.

It is important not to close off our vision from others, believing that our perspective is the only one that matters.

You don't know that.

Each of us is just one camera among many, each offering different angles and insights.

Recognizing and appreciating these diverse points of view can lead to a more comprehensive understanding of the world.

This collective vision is far more powerful than any single perspective. One day, our individual visions will converge into a unified perspective.

When that happens, humanity will be able to live in a true reality where we fully comprehend that all is interconnected and each part is essential to the whole.

This collective awareness will foster a deep sense of unity and belonging among all people, transcending individual differences and conflicts.

WORDS OF WAID

For this future, where true love and understanding among all human beings become the norm, I live today.

By striving to embrace and share different visions, we contribute to the creation of a world where harmony, peace and unity prevail.

It is this hope and commitment to a shared reality that motivates us to live with open hearts and minds, working towards a brighter, more inclusive future.

BE MINDFUL OF YOUR WISHES

Be mindful of what you wish for, as the power of the human mind can bring those desires to fruition.

According to the Teachings of Creation, our thoughts have an incredible ability to manifest into reality.

This shows the importance of being aware and intentional with our wishes.

The human mind holds immense power, a power we are only beginning to understand and harness.

Thoughts, when concentrated and focused, shape our experiences and the world around us.

I can use myself writing this book for example. I thought it; therefore, I manifest it.

This ability to influence reality through thought is a testament to the latent potential within each of us.

We have just begun to scratch the surface of our mental capabilities.

As we continue to explore and understand the might of our thoughts, we uncover new possibilities for personal and collective growth.

This journey into the depths of our mental potential reveals the importance of cultivating positive and constructive thinking.

THE UNIVERSE

The universe is a vast playground for humanity to explore and manipulate, yet humans remain largely ignorant of how to do so

Much like toddlers who have just learned to walk, we are in the early stages of understanding our own capabilities.

We have only recently begun to grasp the immense potential at our disposal.

In or development, we have made significant strides in mastering the physical aspects of existence.

Technological advancements and scientific discoveries have propelled humanity forward, allowing for incredible feats in medicine, engineering, and space exploration.

However, this mastery of the physical world is just one piece of a much larger puzzle. The New Age presents a different aspect.

This understanding is still in its infancy, but true mastery lies beyond the physical realm.

As we begin to tap into this spiritual power, we will unlock deeper insights and capabilities, enabling us to interact with the universe in ways previously thought impossible.

Time travel in the future will become a reality, as Billy himself has experienced countless times.

THE AWAKENING OF THE EGO

The awakening of the ego is a profound transformation. As above, so is below.

When humans achieve a 100% brain quotient, the Creation Energy within them awakens and transcends the cycle of reincarnation.

This marks an evolution, as the Creation Energy no longer needs to reincarnate into human bodies, having reached a higher state of existence.

Similarly, the awakening of the ego occurs through a deep connection with the subconscious mind via the Overall Consciousness Block.

When this connection is fully established, it results in a significant shift in the human being's personality or ego.

The material consciousness, once able to connect with the subconsciousness - where all past wisdom and knowledge are stored - becomes liberated and gains mastery over itself, leading to a heightened sense of self-awareness and autonomy.

This moment of greater understanding is what I refer to as the awakening of the ego.

It represents the point at which an individual's personality transcends its previous limitations and attains true freedom.

This awakening marks the beginning of a new journey, where the ego, now fully conscious and self-directed, navigates its existence with greater clarity and purpose.

Embracing Our Individual racial Identities

Embracing our individual racial identities is crucial for self-acceptance and appreciating cultural diversity.

Every race has its own unique beauty, and no one should ever feel ashamed of who they are.

Historically, many races, including mine, the black race, have faced systemic oppression and discrimination, necessitating movements like "Black I'm Proud" and Black Lives Matter.

It's important to acknowledge that all lives matter and recognize our shared humanity.

However, through these movements, we collectively learn about equality and the destructive power of ignorance.

As we progress, it is my hope that we will reunite as a unified human race, transcending the racial barriers that have divided us for centuries.

The ultimate battle we face is against ignorance itself.

By focusing on education and dismantling belief systems that perpetuate racism, we can move closer to a world free from discrimination.

Our race does not define our worth or superiority. It is merely a part of our identity.

We ought to also know that any race, given the same historical advantages as the white race, could have abused their power similarly.

We must dispel the notion of a superior race or a god that favors one race over others because such truly does not exist.

Addressing racism requires tackling the core issues rather than perpetuating chaos or engaging in racial conflict.

Unfortunately, it sometimes feels like we are nearing a point of no return.

Amidst these challenges, it's important to recognize that most Black people, like myself, strive for equality among all races.

We want everyone to take pride in their racial identity without believing it makes them superior.

In our current times, peace is what most people desire, but those in positions of power often have conflicting interests.

This is why it's crucial to exercise our right to vote and elect leaders who genuinely prioritize peace and equality for all.

Thank you for taking the time to read my thoughts.

Let us continue to work together towards a world where every race is respected and valued.

We are all part of one human race.

When we truly embrace this, there shall be peace on Earth.

Ignore The Things You Can't Change

The more the mind ignores the things it can not change, the more peaceful the human becomes.

This approach emphasizes the importance of focusing our mental energy on factors within our control.

By consciously disregarding uncontrollable circumstances, we can significantly reduce stress and anxiety, leading to a more serene mental state.

Human nature often drives us to seek control over every aspect of our lives, which can result in frustration and mental fatigue.

Many external factors are simply beyond our influence, and attempting to manage them is both futile and exhausting.

Accepting this reality allows us to redirect our efforts toward areas where we can make a meaningful impact.

This mindset aligns with the Teachings, which advocate for distinguishing between what we can and can not control.

As Billy himself said: "If there is a stone in my path, I lift it away, but if it is too heavy, I go around it.

By embracing this perspective, we can cultivate resilience, love and emotional stability, ultimately fostering a more peaceful and fulfilling existence.

HEAVEN

Believing in Heaven, especially one that exists alongside Hell to me, presents profound moral dilemmas.

The idea of living in eternal bliss while knowing that loved ones may be suffering in Hell is deeply unsettling.

How could one find true happiness while aware that a parent, child, or partner is enduring endless torment?

Heaven, under these conditions, to me, is not the paradise it is depicted as.

The emotional and psychological impact of such a belief is significant.

The notion of experiencing everlasting joy while cognizant of the suffering of loved ones appears both impossible and morally troubling.

If the suffering of those close to us is known, the supposed joy of Heaven will logically be marred by feelings of guilt and sorrow.

Thus making Heaven a living hell.

Religion encourages acceptance of doctrines without critical examination, potentially leading to intellectual complacency.

By discouraging questioning, it prevents followers from grappling with diffcult and uncomfortable questions.

The logical inconsistencies in religious beliefs, such as the coexistence of Heaven and Hell, are frequently overlooked to maintain faith.

However, if people were to scrutinize these beliefs more closely, they might find them to be fundamentally illogical and ethically problematic.

Promoting independent thought leads to a deeper understanding of the ethical and logical challenges posed by religious doctrines.

By critically examining these beliefs, people can recognize their inconsistencies and moral issues.

This shift from unquestioning faith to thoughtful analysis fosters a more nuanced and compassionate perspective, potentially leading to the rejection of beliefs that are inherently contradictory and troubling.

The Creation Energy Teachings, with its truth, help human beings to truly see life as it is and not to follow nonsense that brings them only angst.

The Way We Treat Others

The actions we take towards others mirror back on us, highlighting the interconnected nature of human relationships.

When we extend kindness, compassion, or support to others, we not only improve their lives but also enhance our own well-being.

This is because positive actions tend to foster goodwill, strengthen bonds, and create a supportive environment that we are a part of.

Conversely, negative behaviors such as cruelty, indifference, or malice lead to a toxic atmosphere, ultimately affecting our mental and emotional health.

Empathy plays a crucial role in understanding this dynamic.

By putting ourselves in others' shoes, we gain insights into their feelings and experiences, which can guide us to treat them with the respect and consideration we desire for ourselves.

This mutual respect fosters a sense of community and belonging, where each person feels valued and understood.

The empathy we show others comes back to us in times of need, creating a cycle of mutual support and understanding

Moreover, the principle of reciprocity governs human interactions

The way we treat others sets a precedent for how we are treated in return.

Acts of kindness and generosity encourage similar responses from those around us, creating a positive feedback loop.

245

On the other hand, if we treat others poorly, it is likely to breed resentment and negative reactions, which isolate us and lead to a cycle of negativity and conflict.

In essence, our interactions with others reflect back on us, shaping our own experiences and well-being.

By fostering positive relationships and treating others with kindness, we not only uplift those around us but also enhance our own lives.

Recognizing this will inspire us to be more mindful of our actions and their broader implications, ultimately leading to a more harmonious and fulfilling existence.

My Life

My life is like an open book, available for everyone to see.

Each detail about me is laid out transparently on these pages, offering a clear view of my world.

This openness is a conscious choice to promote connection and understanding among those who read my story.

By sharing openly, I invite others to explore and connect with my journey.

This transparency allows people to delve into my experiences and perspectives, fostering a deeper sense of empathy.

By revealing my true self, I can build stronger, more authentic relationships with those around me.

Living this way enables my fellow human beings to truly know me as I am.

It breaks down the barriers that often prevent genuine understanding, encouraging others to see the real person behind the words.

This honest approach helps create a sense of unity and belonging.

In the end, my goal is to cultivate peace and harmony through this openness.

By being transparent and authentic, I hope to inspire others to do the same, creating a community based on mutual respect and genuine connections.

WORDS OF WAID

This way of living not only enriches life but also contributes to a more understanding and compassionate world.

TRUE LOVE

Understanding that everyone is simply a different version of yourself is a profound realization.

This perspective shifts your interactions and relationships, fostering empathy and compassion.

When you see others as reflections of your own experiences, struggles, and emotions, you connect on a deeper level.

This realization leads to true love, as it transcends superficial differences and embraces the shared humanity that binds us all.

Recognizing the commonalities in our existence dissolves barriers and nurtures a sense of unity.

It encourages you to treat others with kindness and understanding, as you would yourself.

Embracing this truth transforms your approach to life and relationships.

It instills a sense of interconnectedness and mutual respect, making it easier to forgive, support, and love others.

True love emerges from this understanding, as it is rooted in empathy and a recognition of our shared human experience.

True love is the realization that, truly, all is one.

Who Was I in Past Lives?

"Who was I in past lives" is a question that most people wonder about after realizing the truth of their immortality and the fact of reincarnation.

However, it doesn't really matter what your past lives were. What matters is only this life.

Your past lives, no matter their nature or significance, are not the focus, and you shouldn't care about them.

What truly matters is the life you are living now.

Each moment and decision in this current existence holds the key to your growth and fulfillment.

The wisdom and knowledge accumulated from your past lives are embedded deep within your subconsciousness.

This vast reservoir of experience shapes your instincts, intuition, and latent abilities. Though these memories are not easily accessible consciously, they influence your present life in subtle and profound ways.

Accessing the insights from your past lives is achievable through the Creation Energy Teachings of Billy Meier.

While your past lives contribute to who you are, it is your actions and choices in this life that define you.

WITHIN THE FABRIC OF REALITY

Each human being perceives reality through the lens of their beliefs.

However, amidst these subjective interpretations, there exists only one singular objective reality.

Billy's Creation Energy Teachings offer a profound insight into this truth, like a blooming spring flower revealing the essence of existence.

By embracing these teachings, individuals begin to unravel the mysteries of life, finding clarity and purpose as they recognize their role as the architects of their own destinies.

Within the realm of diverse beliefs and perspectives, Billy's teachings serve as a BEAM light, illuminating the path toward understanding the fundamental nature of reality.

Like a beacon in the darkness, these teachings empower individuals to discern truth from illusion, fostering a deeper connection to the underlying fabric of reality.

Through this newfound awareness, life's complexities begin to align, allowing individuals to navigate their experiences with clarity and intention.

As people delve deeper into the principles of Creation Energy, they embark on a journey of self-discovery and empowerment.

By acknowledging their inherent capacity to shape reality, they reclaim agency over their lives, transcending limitations and embracing the boundless potential within.

Through these teachings' transformative power, each person has the opportunity to embark on a personal journey towards understanding life, unlocking its mysteries, and crafting their individual path within the fabric of reality.

HUMANITY IS SUMMONED

Humanity is summoned to heed an urgent call, a message resonating across epochs. Let it imprint itself deeply within our souls, a steadfast beacon illuminating our eternal essence.

We are entities tethered to eternity, having traversed myriad lifetimes prior to this existence, with countless more awaiting us in the future.

Let this profound awareness steer us towards embracing the undeniable verity of our intrinsic interconnectedness, weaving together as a unified collective, the Human race.

In acknowledging this timeless truth, we recognize our shared journey through the annals of time, interconnected threads weaving the fabric of our collective experience. Each soul is a luminary in the vast expanse of existence and contributes its unique hue to the tapestry of humanity.

As we embrace this realization, we foster empathy, compassion, and solidarity, transcending the boundaries that divide us and uniting in the essence of our shared humanity.

Let us forge ahead with this profound understanding as our guiding light, navigating the complexities of existence with grace and unity. In embracing our interconnectedness, we honor the sanctity of life itself, weaving a narrative of compassion, understanding, and coexistence.

Together, let us embark on this journey, bound by the eternal tapestry of our shared human experience.

WHEN CRITICIZING RELIGION

When criticizing religion, it's important to avoid targeting people for their beliefs.

Everyone has the right to their own faith, and this personal choice should be respected.

Making fun of someone's prayers or expressions of gratitude to their God is disrespectful and will lead to unpeace and disharmony.

My critiques are always directed at the institutions of religion, not the people who practice them.

I recognize that many people are indoctrinated from a young age, much like I was.

This understanding informs my approach, ensuring I focus on the broader structures rather than the believers themselves.

It's crucial to maintain a compassionate perspective when discussing religion.

Recognizing the influence of upbringing and societal pressures on a person's beliefs helps foster empathy.

Attacking people for their choices is counterproductive and fails to address the root issues within religious institutions.

Always try to remember, people are not really dumb and stupid for believing in God.

The God belief itself has become a mental disease in the brain of the human being. They really can not help themselves unless they want to help themselves.

BAD ENERGY

People who harbor feelings of anger, envy, jealousy, resentment, vengeance, and rage experience significant unhappiness.

Their negative emotions cloud their judgment and interactions, leading to a pervasive sense of dissatisfaction and discontent.

Such negativity is both harmful to themselves and to those around them.

It is essential to protect your own well-being from these human beings.

Their toxic energy can easily seep into your life, affecting your mood and overall happiness.

Being mindful of their influence and setting boundaries is crucial to maintaining your peace and positivity.

Recognizing when to distance yourself from negative energy is key.

Walking away from toxic situations or people is not a sign of weakness but a necessary step to safeguard your mental and emotional health.

Prioritizing your inner peace by avoiding those who consistently bring negativity into your life is not only recommended, but I'm also a client.

Recognizing reality

Recognizing reality presents a profound challenge in life, demanding the courage to confront our biases and embrace perspectives that diverge from our own. It requires a willingness to let go of preconceived notions and acknowledge the complexity inherent in our understanding of the world.

Central to this process is the realization that reality is multifaceted, shaped by individual experiences and interpretations. By respecting and valuing diverse perspectives, we foster an environment of mutual understanding and harmony.

Honesty and transparency are essential in navigating the complexities of shared reality. By speaking our minds openly and honestly, we create opportunities for genuine communication and understanding.

This commitment to authenticity helps prevent misunderstandings and fosters trust and respect in our relationships.

In the pursuit of acknowledging reality, we are called to engage in dialogue with humility and empathy. It requires a willingness to challenge our assumptions and confront discomfort in order to broaden our understanding of the world.

By embracing the diversity of human experience, we move towards a more inclusive and compassionate appreciation of reality.

Disgusted By

If you find yourself disgusted by witnessing two men or two women kissing, it's important to recognize that the source of that disgust lies within your own feelings and beliefs, rather than in the act of kissing itself.

The expression of affection between two human beings should not inherently provoke feelings of disgust, as it is a natural display of human emotion and connection.

To label such an act as disgusting re ects a personal reaction influenced by societal norms or personal biases.

Therefore, your perception of two homosexuals kissing as disgusting is rooted in your own internalized judgments and prejudices rather than any objective measure of the act itself.

It is crucial to separate personal discomfort or societal conditioning from the genuine expression of love and affection between people.

Critically examining why such feelings arise can lead to greater understanding and empathy towards diverse forms of human relationships.

Recognize the fact that two human beings kissing regardless whether they're the same gender or not is not at all disgusting may help some people grasp the importance of tolerance, acceptance, and respect for individuals' rights to express their love freely.

It also challenges individuals to confront and reconsider their own biases and prejudices, promoting a more inclusive and compassionate outlook on human diversity and relationships.

WORDS OF WAID

This simple act of understanding helps to promote peace and harmony amongst human beings

THE CANVAS OF OUR EXISTENCE

Mastering the art of controlling our thoughts sets the stage for dictating our actions, thus influencing the trajectory of our lives.

By harnessing the power of our minds, we can navigate freely through challenges of life.

This control over our thoughts empowers us to make conscious choices, steering us towards positive outcomes and personal growth.

In the journey of life, we become the architects of our own experiences, weaving the intricate tapestry of lessons that shape our understanding and character.

Every decision, whether small or significant, contributes to the narrative of our existence.

As both writers and actors in this grand theater of life, we hold the pen to script our stories and the responsibility to bring them to life through our actions.

Embracing the dual roles of creator and protagonist, we embark on a quest of self-discovery and fulfillment.

With each chapter we write and every scene we perform, we mold the substance of our reality.

Through introspection and intentional living, we can craft a life rich in meaning, purpose, and authenticity.

As we continue to evolve, we recognize the profound impact of our thoughts and actions in shaping the canvas of our existence.

This book is a testimony to how the Teachings of the Creation Energy have profoundly transformed my inner being.

259

WORDS OF WAID

Through the wisdom and guidance shared within these pages, I have found a new way of living that resonates deeply with my core essence.

The experiences and insights I offer here are a reflection of my personal journey and the perspective I have developed in navigating life's many challenges and connections with others.

It is important to clarify that I am not suggesting that my way is the only or correct way for everyone.

No one has the authority to dictate how another person should live or act.

However, the principles I follow have brought me a sense of peace and harmony, which I feel compelled to share.

By living in accordance with the Teachings of the Creation Energy, I have discovered a fulfilling and balanced approach to life.

My life is now aligned with the laws and recommendations of Creation, a path I find to be deeply rewarding and enriching.

This alignment has brought me a profound sense of inner peace and clarity, which I hope to convey through the pages of this book.

The advice and reflections contained herein are meant to inspire and offer a different perspective, not to prescribe a specific way of living.

SEPARATE WAYS

If someone decides they don't want to be with you, it's important not to internalize it as a personal rejection.

Everyone has their own preferences and reasons for their choices, which may not always align with your own.

Instead of dwelling on it, it's healthier to accept their decision gracefully.

Respect their autonomy and allow them the space to make choices that are best for them, even if it differs from what you desire.

Attempting to force someone to reciprocate your feelings or stay in a relationship against their will is counterproductive.

It not only disregards their feelings but also disrupts the natural harmony between individuals.

Relationships thrive on mutual respect and consent, and any attempt to coerce or manipulate undermines these fundamental principles.

True connection cannot be forced.

It must be willingly embraced by both parties.

Respecting someone's choices demonstrates maturity and empathy.

It shows that you value their autonomy and emotional well-being above your own desires.

WORDS OF WAID

By honoring their decisions, you cultivate a healthier environment for both yourself and the other person, fostering mutual respect and understanding in all your interactions.

Everyone is on their own journey.

True love is to allow others their freedom to choose and to go through their own journey without any guilt.

FORGIVING THOSE WHO WRONGED YOU

Forgiving those who have wronged you is a powerful act that can lead to absolute inner peace.

When you release the burden of resentment and anger, you free yourself from the emotional weight that holds you back.

Forgiveness is not about condoning or excusing the actions of others but rather about choosing to let go of the negative energy that is consuming you.

By forgiving others, you reclaim your power and take control of your own happiness.

Holding onto grudges only perpetuates feelings of bitterness and resentment, trapping you in a cycle of negativity.

When you choose to forgive, you break free from this cycle and open yourself up to a sense of liberation and tranquility.

Forgiveness is also an act of self-love and compassion.

When you forgive someone, you acknowledge your own worth and refuse to let their actions define your sense of self.

Instead of allowing anger and resentment to poison your well being, you choose to cultivate feelings of kindness and understanding, both towards others and towards yourself.

In the end, forgiveness is not just about letting go of the past.

It's about creating a brighter future.

WORDS OF WAID

When you forgive those who have wronged you, you pave the way for healing and growth, both personally and in your relationships with others.

By embracing forgiveness, you open yourself up to a life filled with peace, joy, and fulfillment.

DEDICATIONS

This book is dedicated to Billy Meier, the Goblet of the Truth. His teachings have been instrumental in guiding me towards a better and harmonious existence. It is my hope that readers will find value in these teachings and perhaps see their own lives in a new light, as I have through this journey.